THE YEAR IT ALL MADE SENSE

David Alfred George

INCREDIBLE
publishing

Hampstead, NH

Copyright © 2016 by David Alfred George
Incredible Publishing
All rights reserved. Published in the United States of America.
Printed in the United States of America.
Incredible Publishing
New Hampshire, USA
www.TheYearItAllMadeSense.com

Cover design by Derek Wakeen
Cover photograph by Shane Wakeen
Chapter drawings by Derek Wakeen
Interior design by Kevin Callahan / BNGO Books
Video editing by Jeffrey McGurren (video e-book)
Music produced by Brix Sound Lab (video e-book)

This is a work of non-fiction. All rights reserved. All content in this book is based on true events. No part of this publication may be reproduced, stored in a retrieval system, or transmitted in any form or by any means—for example, electronic, photocopy, recording—without the prior written permission of the publisher, except by a reviewer who may quote brief passages in a review.

Library of Congress Control Number: 2016905736

George, David A.,1983-, author
The Year It All It Made Sense / written by David Alfred George.

Issued in print and electronic formats.
ISBN 978-0-9974644-0-5 (pbk.)
ISBN 978-0-9974644-1-2 (epub)
ISBN 978-0-9974644-2-9 (video e-book)
ISBN 978-0-9974644-3-6 (pdf)
ISBN 978-0-9974644-4-3 (audio)

For Ava D. & Kiana

For Ava D. & Kiana

Contents

Prologue

You might be asking yourself, "Why spend my time reading this?"

Why invest in somebody else's life story? I don't have that answer. But I do know that I'm passionate about every venture I have ever faced in my life while thriving on words like *risk*, *try*, *observe*, *interact*, *experience*, *laugh*, *learn*, *grow*, and most of all *change*.

Growing up I had the privilege of watching the lifestyle of three family writers: Mark, Peter, and Paul were home inspectors in the New England territory of the United States. At a young age, I had no real idea what my father, Paul, did when he left the house for work besides what he had told me. He explained that he had to write a report on everything he saw throughout his day while looking at houses, buildings, and all different structures. The goal was to write down descriptions of what he saw and to be clear, covering everything that was wrong with each dwelling that he passed through in his workday. He had to be careful because if the buyer purchased what was inspected and something went wrong that wasn't mentioned in the report, then the inspector could be sued. I learned quickly from my father that the only difference between a lawyer and a bucket of shit was the bucket!

I spent a lot of childhood moments at my uncle Mark's home and my uncle Peter's home. All three brothers, Mark, Peter, and Paul, had a home office that was furnished and decorated to their own style. I would watch each one of them sit quietly behind their desks writing with pen and paper. To me, as a young child, that was their work. They would sit in the comfort of their home surrounded by their family and write. The lifestyle I observed and witnessed growing up is what I was attracted to.

Ricky Roy was my mother's brother and also the man I idolized most in life because all he ever did was tell stories and laugh. He would almost never address me by my first name either; he always called me "Pilgrim." Once when we were driving down the road in a beat-up dark-green dump truck that delivered firewood and wood chips, he said to me, "Pilgrim! I wish that I could retire at thirty-five and live a simple life." I asked him, "What would you do with your time?" He replied, "I would have fun! It would really put the *J* in joy."

He began to slow the truck down to almost a stop at the top of a hill in Derry, New Hampshire, and said, "Pilgrim, roll down your window." He leaned over. "Pilgrim, you see this old farmhouse? That is where Robert Frost lived! He was a famous writer. Look how beautiful and peaceful his property is." Then he stepped on the gas and told me to roll my window up. "How great would that be, huh?" he said. "Live in an old farmhouse, take care of your property, hunt right in your backyard, and write about how you see the world. That would put the *J* in joy for sure." He continued to drive down the road, transitioning from an absolute high to a sad face, as if the *J* wasn't even there.

Ricky Roy was an American lumberjack who had a passion for the outdoors. He worked the New England area as a professional tree climber. To me, his work was a way to gain a passion for the outdoors while not only watching the change of each season, year after year, from up in a tree, but from actually being a part of it. Most of us have been taught that if we allow nature to take its course, then success will follow.

Each one of these men said something to me out of what could have been wisdom, experience, regret, or maybe something that they truly believed. My father, Paul George, once said, "David! Make sure you do everything you say you're going to do in life!" My uncle Mark George once said, "Work will mess up your entire life!" My uncle Peter George once said, "You're only going to be successful if you do what you enjoy in life!" My uncle Ricky Roy said repeatedly, **"Sky's the limit, Pilgrim!"** at the end of almost every conversation.

After letting each phrase sink into my head at a young age, from the people I loved and respected dearly, I made a decision to create a lifestyle built off of their words of inspiration.

Chapter One

Spinning Out of Control

When I was in the first grade, my father dropped me off at the beginning of the school year. After he gave me a hug and a kiss, I hopped out of his truck and started walking toward the building. There was an older kid at school, Andrew. He happened to be outside that morning, and as I approached where he was standing against the building, he spit right in my face and then ran away, acting like a fool. As I took my glasses off and started to wipe them clean, my father's voice bellowed across the school yard. "David, get over here now!"

As soon as I got to his truck, he asked me, "Did that kid spit in your face?" After I said yes, he took one look at me, paused, and said, "You walk back up there right now, clench your fist, and punch that kid as hard as you can right in the middle of his face. Do you understand me?!" I made a slow nod and said, "OK." I proceeded to walk right toward Andrew. As I came closer and closer, he locked eyes with me, and without saying anything at all, once I was in arm's reach, I cracked him as hard as I could in the middle of his nose! He fell to the ground. I turned to look back at my father, and he had a big grin from ear to ear plastered on his face. He gave me a thumbs-up and drove away!

I was born in 1983 in a small state on the East Coast that uses three words in its slogan: "Make It Yours." I grew up in a middle-class family and was preached to as if it were a Catholic household. One phrase that held significant weight in my childhood home was "Don't ever be a sheep in life." Those words have been ingrained into my brain, going back to my earliest memories. My father would look me straight in the eyes and say over and over, **"David, don't you ever be a sheep in life! Do you understand me? You stay out of the herd always!"** Most of the time he had both hands on my shoulders, with a solid shake signifying the punctuation at the end of each sentence.

I was never that great of a student. Actually, if there is one word in the world that makes me cringe more than anything, it's the word *school*. I grew up getting pulled out of classes and brought down to the special education rooms. I was laughed at quite often for needing extra help. I remember thinking to myself,

"What is everyone who's laughing doing in life that allows *them* to laugh at *me*?"

The one and only thing I did enjoy in school was observing everyone around me. I watched teachers, principals, janitors, lunch ladies, crossing guards, and anyone and everyone who was doing something different than receiving a report card. As much as the word *school* made me cringe, I had a fascination with the word *learn*, while observing the world around me. *That* was my favorite part of school.

Another piece of advice that was driven into my mind as a child was to plan on working for yourself in life. I was told there was a lot of money in this world with a myriad of ways to get ahold of it. There was no reason to roll your sleeves up and go to work, putting everything you're made of on the line, to improve the wealth of somebody else's life. I was taught three things in business: to be a boss, to respect everyone, and to know that life is not fair so you better get fucking used to it. And if you don't like it, then you better figure out a way to fix it.

Once I got to high school, I had absolutely no interest in anything the teachers had to say. I figured I might as well use my time wisely and get involved with something I could benefit from while attending high school. I started to realize that there were many students who enjoyed spending their money on drugs. Work for yourself? Sounded good to me!

I was addicted to the adrenaline rush of doing something illegal. School was no longer a waste of my time. The crazy thing is, it made me smile a true smile each day. I got so involved in drug dealing that I stopped carrying school books at all. By junior year, I had finally convinced the school board that I was fit for their work-release program. I found myself wandering throughout the school building to burn off time or sleeping in class. Most of the time I would be woken up by either the teacher or a loud noise that sent me into a confused but enjoyable awakening before it was time to head out into the working world. Each school day finished up for me at ten thirty, and I would head up north to fire up a chainsaw and start bucking up logs to split them into firewood. The one thing I have always enjoyed was putting in some good, hard work to fulfill each day. It made me feel free.

By age eighteen, I had flunked out of English class; I'm pretty sure it was because I chose not to even show up. As a result, I couldn't finish up my last year playing ice hockey. This happened to be the season that was documented for the true story *Ice Time*, written by Jay Atkinson, who followed all the players around during practice and games and even sat in classrooms and at the lunch tables with a note pad, taking in whatever he wanted. It was one of the most interesting jobs I had ever seen before—he was observing everything and everyone in his path. I hung my head low and listened to the author tell me how I ought to be ashamed of myself about missing the hockey season.

Shortly afterward I was kicked out of school for a combination of fighting and drugs. The school was tired of my behavior. It was not the first time I had acted that way on their grounds, and they knew the kind of extracurricular activities I was involved with as well. I can remember looking down at the person I had punched in the face many times with rights and lefts—a fight that got me expelled from high school. He was looking up at me as blood was dripping from his face. I had his blood on my fist, and I began wiping off the back of my hand on his dazed face while saying, "Here, take your blood back." Then I walked away with a smile on my face, ready to attack my next challenge.

Looking back, I was out of control. Something was wrong with me. But whether it was good or bad, right or wrong, I swore I was going at it with my head held high, and my chest out, as I followed my heart!

At nineteen I started taking traditional karate. Street fighting was no longer attractive to me, and I was now falling in love with the art of using my body as a weapon to strengthen the mind and, more so, self-discipline. Traditional karate was not the only thing I was falling in love with however. I was falling in love with a girl named Danielle.

I've known Danielle since we were kids. My close cousins grew up in the same neighborhood as Danielle. I knew her name but that was about it. I saw her for years, splashing around in a brook that ran through the neighborhood, riding our bikes down the backstreets, making eye contact in the hallway at school, passing shoulder to shoulder at parties; it went on and on without us ever exchanging many words with one another but always smiling.

Love at first sight exists! In 2006, Danielle and I moved up north and bought an old farmhouse built in 1870. I had now accomplished a vision that I had been cherishing from my youth. The day that I drove by Robert Frost's farm and listened to my uncle explain how great it would be to live in an old farmhouse and take care of your property was no longer a childhood fantasy but a dream come true. The property sat on ten acres. Danielle and I had sold off seven acres and now had a beautiful home with the comfort of equity right from the start. We spent two years gutting the house and making it our own. That was where we would have our life together.

The first time the realtor brought Danielle and I through the home, we ended up in the fourth bedroom. I leaned up against the back window like I was looking out and unlocked the window latch so I could sneak back in to my future home and brainstorm about my life without the realtor standing by my side. Danielle and I snuck in a few times during the next few weeks before we even had a closing date. She and I sat at the kitchen table one night, laughing and talking with no urgency to leave.

It was like we had already moved in!

Then on June 7, 2008, Danielle and I said "I DO!" We stood in front of the most interesting human being I have ever known—David Sollars. Mr. Sollars wed us that beautiful day on Meredith Bay, with the sun shining brightly over Lake Winnipesaukee. Danielle and I became Mr. and Mrs. George, and we were both eager to start a family. Our first daughter, Ava Dorothy George, was born twelve months later in 2009.

During those years, and in the years that followed, I began mixed martial arts (MMA) training. The art of fighting truly trickled through my veins, and it was hard to shut that feeling off. The thrill of testing myself and other people seemed to satisfy that feeling I longed for. Given that I held a certain reputation since that first punch in the first grade, I thought I might as well keep that lifestyle going.

I fought three fights for an organization called Combat Zone MMA. This was a fight league that produced shows in Massachusetts and New Hampshire, introducing some of New England's best local fighters, such as Calvin "the Boston Finisher" Kattar, UFC's Kenny "KenFlo" Florian, Marcus "the Hand Grenade" Davis, Joe "J-Lau" Lauzon, John "Doomsday" Howard, and many more. I had won my first two fights as an MMA competitor. As time continued, I started to talk a lot about the business side of the fight game with my coach, and he told me to focus on fighting. Shortly thereafter, I booked a third fight with Combat Zone MMA, and my coach confronted me and said, "David, the owner of Combat Zone MMA is in a financial jam. Would you have any interest in having me set up a meeting with him?" I said, "Yes!"

I purchased the fight league and turned Combat Zone MMA into a limited liability company. I began organizing events, starting with the bout on October 13, 2007, that I was already scheduled to fight in. The fight did not, however, end the way I had planned. I ended up cutting a check to UFC's veteran, Danny "the Upgrade" Lauzon, for defeating me inside a cage in front of all my family and friends on my first promotion ever in the fight business. Danny had me in a high mount, laying leather into my face, punch after punch. When I got out of the cage and finally recomposed myself, my coach started laughing his ass off and told me that my legs were flaring around in the air as I tried to escape from my beatdown. He said, "You looked like a French whore getting pounded out!" Like I said, it did not end the way I had planned! But I was now on a new path in the fight game while ending my short-lived fighting career with a 2-1-0 record.

I snapped into business mode and struck a deal with Rockingham Park, a horse-racing track in Salem, New Hampshire, where ESPN held boxing events. This was also a home at one point for boxing champion Micky Ward, as portrayed in the Hollywood film *The Fighter*. I had a good feeling and vibe coming in my direction the first time I stepped foot in the event room, knowing that good things had already happened in the fight world under those lights. The track gave me an exclusive deal, and I was ready to start making a living promoting four live cage-fighting events a year! The thrill of this new line of work was the art of instigation, getting two humans to fight it out like warriors inside a cage.

I was simultaneously working as a full-time lumberjack, mostly as a professional tree climber in the industry. I put myself in a tree for the first time at sixteen years old and never looked down! I decided it was time to move up and look at the world from a high point and to actually start living that passion for the outdoors that I had witnessed in my uncle Ricky Roy after many years of shadowing him as a youth. I also thought a lot about the wise words from my uncle Peter when I was a child. He expressed how you are only successful if you do something that you enjoy. All the tree climbers that I had ever watched seemed as if they were not working. They all looked like they were having a good time and staying fit by pushing themselves to greater heights.

So as a day job, I chose to climb trees for most of my working life because I felt free and at peace. The word *work* that we often hear many people dread did not exist in my daily grind. Once I started running Combat Zone MMA, I backed off the tree industry so I could focus on building up my fight league.

In early 2011, Danielle and I found out that she was pregnant with our second child! Toward the beginning of that summer, I decided to step it up again in the tree industry. My uncle had been asking me for years if I would like to purchase half of his company, which he'd been running for twenty-five years. Maybe it had something to do with him missing his retirement at age thirty-five and bumping down the road in that old green truck. Whatever it was, it didn't matter to me. I had Combat Zone MMA under control, and I had time on my side. So I went for it!

The plan was to go into business with my uncle Ricky Roy, but the company had to make a purchase. That purchase was a crane. I said I would go into business with my uncle under one condition: we open an independent crane service. His company was paying out too much in crane rental fees, so that was the first problem to start fixing. The crane would go out on its own jobs and service other tree companies, which I set up prior to our purchase. We would also use the crane for our own jobs.

Three months later I witnessed erratic behavior from my uncle, the man I idolized, and it turned into the fastest learning experience I had ever lived. I watched him scream and get in a pickup truck to leave and then return. He'd scream some more, leave, and then return again to pout, storm around, and even cry on the job sites. Customers were concerned and called the office to complain, and employees left the company. Midlife crisis or poor behavior, I don't know, but it was unacceptable if I had a financial interest in the company. Because of his behavior, which I wanted no part of, I asked him if he would like to take his company back as full ownership. I had a good thing going with Combat Zone MMA, which allowed me the freedom to drift in a direction other than failure, based on my mindset as a business owner.

My uncle stated that he hated dealing with people, couldn't stand being an owner of a company anymore, and wanted no part of the tree industry. I knew I had two options: walk away from the tree industry like my uncle was doing or capitalize 100 percent on an up-and-running business. I chose more dollar signs, which ultimately increased the thickness of bullshit I had to deal with.

In June 2011, I heard about a casting call for the game show *Survivor.* I'd never even watched the show, but it was my mother's favorite, and she had never missed an episode. It sounded like a challenge, and I was up for it! Most of my drive came from my mother repeatedly saying, "David, try out for the game show *Survivor*," after she watched the first episode.

Danielle and I didn't have cable since we felt that too much TV seemed to interfere with living a productive lifestyle. I also didn't have Facebook or any other social media platform. I loved my privacy and staying tapped into what I was doing for my own satisfaction. I thought that if I gave *Survivor* a shot, it would be a thrill for my mother to watch her son on her favorite TV game show, but I would have to break through a lot of roadblocks I had built up for myself over the years when it came to privacy.

I gave my childhood friend Jeff McGurren a call. His expertise was video editing. We started working on the three-and-a-half-minute casting video. At the start, I screamed out loud, **"I am the next survivor!"** I repeated that line again at the end of the video and repeated it to myself daily. I started daydreaming about entering the world of entertainment throughout the country. It was a chance for millions of viewers to sit back in the comfort of their homes and watch my behavior in a game built off of athleticism and twisted together with mind-manipulating strategies to gain self-gratification. All of this in hopes of being rewarded with first place in a survival game.

The phrase my father had once said to me about how important it was to do everything you say you're going to do in life had once again come into play. After watching the casting video, the only part that became real to me was the beginning and the end, where I screamed, "I AM THE NEXT SURVIVOR." Not only did I verbalize what I was going to do, I had the privilege of watching it over and over again, reassuring myself that I had said it. Jeff even posted the video on YouTube to market his work.

However, deep down inside, I knew that rolling the dice to possibly make it on a TV show would pull me away from my two-year-old daughter and pregnant wife. It did not look so good from the outside in. I felt selfish but was able to walk past that feeling because I knew the strength inside of Danielle. She and I agreed that the most important value we could ever share with our children was not telling them but showing them that they can truly do anything in life if they wanted it bad enough, by living through the experience and making it real.

Since becoming a father, my main goal was to teach my young that life was about having fun, and when time runs out, your smile would show that you DID IT! YOU DID EVERYTHING YOU EVER WANTED TO DO IN LIFE! Try not to listen to that sad poor-me story about why you couldn't accomplish something. Tell yourself "I can" every day! That was what I believed was important to pass on to the children of our future. So, in September, Jeff and I mailed out the video and began the waiting game. I was told twenty thousand to thirty thousand videos would be submitted. I sat back and hoped luck would be on my side. In the meantime, I was back to the fast-paced, crazy lifestyle of working seven days a week.

On November 18, our second little miracle arrived into our lives. Ava Dorothy George had a baby sister. Danielle and I looked at her sticky little eyes trying to open and close and then gave her a name, Kiana George.

Winter came up fast that year in New England. Typically, tree work slowed down a bit in the colder months, but at the beginning of December, we were still working long, hard days. On Thursday,

December 1, 2011, I fell out of a spruce tree. I had been climbing for twelve years, and it was the first time I ever fell. I came down hard on my right ankle. I finished up the workday and stopped at a hospital on my way home, to make sure there was no break in my ankle. After the x-rays showed no break, I walked out of the ER with a wrapped-up, swollen ankle, feeling pretty lucky about my day. It forced me to take some time off from climbing for a few days, and it was nice to actually sit down in my home and enjoy my family. It's sad that it took a fall out of a spruce tree for me to slow down my work life to spend time with Danielle and our two little girls.

I was back to work on Monday, December 5. That night, after Danielle and I put the girls to sleep, I hopped in the shower. As always, I thoroughly washed myself. But this time, I stopped and paused as I was washing my body, and I called Danielle's name. I said, "Come here!" As she walked into the bathroom, I opened the shower curtain, and standing there under the running water, I asked her to massage my right nut because something wasn't right.

Now Danielle, being a registered nurse at Massachusetts General Hospital in the pediatric ICU, was conditioned to take immediate action on anything health related that raised a red flag. She looked up at my eyes once her hand came in contact with the same hard, knotted-up lump that I had felt. I said, "What is that?" Danielle answered with a nervous look on her face, "I don't know, but please go get it looked at." I didn't think much of it, as I figured I had crushed it when I fell, and it would heal up in no time. But the next night it was still there. Danielle asked me kindly to get an ultrasound done. I agreed.

On December 7, I underwent an ultrasound. Seven days later on December 14, Danielle and I were sitting in the doctor's office, waiting for the results. The door opened and the doctor came bouncing in on his tippy-toes, spunky as ever with a smile on his face. He was a silly little man. After he introduced himself and took a seat, he told me I had a cancerous tumor and that my right testicle had to be removed.

My first thought was "Oh shit, that's fucked up." Then I began to hear Danielle sniffling and saw her wiping tears from her eyes. I reached out and grabbed her knee to comfort her as I stayed focused on the doctor. He gave Danielle his attention and went on to say, "It's no big deal; it's like getting a tooth pulled out! We will do it in the outpatient setting. There's nothing to worry about." I took a deep breath and envisioned myself grabbing the doctor behind the neck and smashing his face off his desk and then yanking out every one of his teeth. Danielle began crying heavily and got up and walked out of the room. I stood up, leaving without a handshake. I grabbed Kiana as I turned away and walked out the door. Danielle and I left with our newborn still sleeping in her car seat. I remember the car seat bouncing off my leg as we walked through the parking lot toward the car, but really, **we were walking toward a completely different direction in our life.**

Before I even had a chance to start the car, Danielle put a call into Mass General, where she worked. She was able to get me an appointment the next day with a new physician, Dr. C, for a second opinion. This Dr. C was a better man to sit and talk with about the new direction life had sent us in. He had a little girl about the same age as our oldest daughter and a second baby girl on the way in a few months. We had a lot in common right away on what mattered most in life. It didn't even matter what his expertise was at that moment because we sat and talked about life. It was a sincere conversation before we spoke about business.

I could see the comfort building in Danielle as we both spoke with him, and that was all I truly cared about.

Bottom line, it was confirmed that the spunky, silly little man who had first diagnosed me was correct: my right nut was about to be chopped off due to cancer! Dr. C informed me I would spend the night at Mass General and would go in for surgery the next day. I shook his hand firmly and said, "OK, Doc. Let's do it."

I can remember lying in my hospital bed, thinking back to when the doctor was explaining possible side effects from the surgery he was about to perform. The only one that I actually remembered was ED—erectile dysfunction. I lay in the bed and thought about it. After brooding over how good sex was for hours and hours, I dropped it and took on the mindset I have had my entire life, and that was to not give a flying fuck about negativity. It was what it was, and life always went on! Fourteen days later, I was a healed man. I still woke up every morning with a hard-on that Danielle could swing from, so I counted my blessings and was grateful for the outcome. I was ready to start a new year.

The next twenty-six days went by in a fast-paced confusion of overloaded workdays. I was playing catch-up for time missed. There was no need to look behind me in the rearview mirror. I was back on the streets scraping up tree work for my crew as a salesman, working as a foreman on my own jobs, running my crane from time to time when I couldn't find an operator to run it for me, and still organizing fights. During this time, one of the reporters from the local newspaper, the *Eagle-Tribune*, had asked if he could write an article about me and about my cage fighting organization. In bold letters, at the start of the article, it read,

"George goes from fighter to promoter!" On that same page, in the top right corner of the article, was a three-word question in all caps: **"WILL HE SURVIVE?"**

That question messed with my head on a number of levels. No one had known about my run-in with cancer. The newspaper reporter had asked at the end of our conversation, "What else is new in your life?" I explained how I was giving the game show *Survivor* a shot. So he wrote about it. It seemed like life was toying with me a little. I kept reading. "Local entrepreneur has the Midas touch!" That line stroked my ego and made me hungry to read more. It continued, "How David George has time to sleep is anyone's guess. **What the twenty-eight-year-old entrepreneur has on his resume would make Steve Jobs blush.**" That was the most humbling experience I had ever had. I wondered, "I don't even know who Steve Jobs is, so why is he blushing?"

When I got to my office, I asked my cousin Melissa George, who was working security, "Who is Steve Jobs?" She looked at me like I was from outer space. She shook her head while laughing and said, "Are you serious?" I replied, "Who the hell is he?" She said, still laughing through her words, "David, he invented Apple! You know, all the devices that the majority of the world buries their faces in. Well, he started it!"

I thought to myself, "WOW!" I quietly walked away from Melissa and sat down at my desk. I began to have a jaw-dropping moment all by myself with a completely clear mind, saying over and over again in my thoughts, "Holy shit. HOLY SHIT!" I gathered up what I had taken out of my briefcase, put it back in, and walked out of the office, telling Melissa that I was going down to Rockingham Park to make sure that the event room was looking good for the fights that night.

I drove away in my truck, but I pulled over on the side of the road after about five minutes. I reached into my briefcase and pulled out the newspaper article. I looked back at the headline: "WILL HE SURVIVE?" Then I scanned right down to the spot where it read "Steve Jobs blush," and I started laughing my ass off as I stuffed the article back in my briefcase.

Within two weeks after the write-up in the paper, my *Survivor* casting video had over four thousand hits. It was mind blowing to see how many people were interested in the video. It was the first time in my life that I saw the power of the Internet. I also realized that I had now told a lot of people what I was going to do next.

My mother had stopped by one night and dropped off a few *Survivor* DVDs of previous seasons and shows. She said she knew I didn't watch it, but she thought maybe I would like to learn a little about the show I might get on. I popped in a DVD one night and watched it for a little bit and then put in another. But that all came to a quick stop when I realized it was about people and challenges! The people changed and so did the challenges. There was nothing else to figure out. It was based on luck, mental skills, and physical abilities.

Things seemed to be falling into place for me, because in February 2012, I found an email waiting in my inbox from Caitlin Moore, a casting agent at *Survivor.* She had sent me a 114-page contract, which she followed up with a phone call. In our conversation, she suggested I watch previous seasons to observe other people's strategies. I told Caitlin I was not going to play like anyone else. I was going to be me. I thought back to when I was watching those DVDs and said to myself, "How will staring at the television help me gain luck or increase mental skills or physical skills? There is nothing to master!" Everything she asked me to view on television as a learning curve was going to change if I got there. I started to believe I had a pretty good shot of making it to the semifinals of the auditions, considering I was one of *Survivor*'s biggest antifans, and I made this clear to Caitlin Moore as well. Along with the contract, there were some medical disclosure forms to fill out to explain my cancer. I got clearance letters from all my doctors and kept moving forward aggressively.

That February a few friends and I had planned a snowboarding trip to Jackson Hole, Wyoming, to spend a few days out in the big country carving down the side of a mountain on a snowboard. I was already stoked as ever, having mailed out the contract before I hopped on the flight. The day before I left for Jackson Hole was Valentine's Day. Danielle had given me a small red bag and inside was a GoPro Hero. It was a small cube-shaped silver video camera. I had never heard of or seen one of these before. She said, "I know you don't care too much about technology, but I figured it would be fun to film your trip."

Once I arrived in Wyoming, I charged the GoPro up and stuck a mount on top of my helmet the next morning before I headed out the door. One of my best childhood friends, Shane Wakeen, also had a GoPro mounted on the top of his helmet. Shane and I and the rest of our group loaded our boards and ourselves on a gondola. The ride up the mountain gave me a moment of clarity. The group of friends I was with started to have a conversation about what a wild idea it would be to film yourself for an entire year with a GoPro and follow yourself day in and day out. My mind took this concept and spun it into a million different directions. I was fascinated with watching the daily routines of people around me, but I had never considered watching myself. Plus, that would also be like having the cameras follow me around if

I made it on the TV show *Survivor*! I thought often about how I would handle the full-time filming if I actually made it on the show. The contract said I would be filmed by a camera crew 24/7. I thought having some GoPro time would be great practice.

Besides using a GoPro for the first time, there was something else that I did for the first time in my life in Jackson Hole while listening to a live band, Green Sky Blue Grass. I purchased their CD! I made it twenty-eight years without coughing up a buck in the music industry until I stepped foot into a barroom in a state that was "Like No Place on Earth."

I returned to Boston, safe and sound from Wyoming, on Sunday, February 19. Once I got back to my homestead in New Hampshire, I lit my wood stoves and spent the next two days rolling around my living room, playing with my family and leaving my cell phone turned off. Then I was back in Boston for my post-surgery follow-up and to get some blood work and x-rays done. The doctor who performed my surgery said my scar looked good, and I seemed to be healing up great.

The next day I got a phone call from the casting agent Caitlin Moore. I was in! She explained that *Survivor* wanted to fly me out to California for the semifinals. At the end of the conversation, Caitlin Moore asked me which airport I would like to fly out of. I told her Boston's Logan International Airport would be great. She also mentioned I would be leaving on March 5. I was told to clear my schedule and await further details.

Two days later on Friday morning, February 24, I got up nice and early, ready to head out and spend the day with Mother Nature up in a tree, feeling free and at peace as a lumberjack. On my way down the stairs, I heard Ava D. wake up, and she started lightly crying. I walked into her room and scooped her up out of the crib. I sat down in the rocking chair and snuggled her, trying to get her to go back to sleep. My cell phone started ringing in my pocket, so I quickly answered it, trying not to disturb Ava D. I figured it was one of the guys calling about the job. It was not. It was the doctor from Mass General, and he had the results back from my blood work.

His voice was calm and low. He said, "I'm sorry to call you so early, but we received your blood work from Tuesday, and it's showing that your cancer is back. You have to come to the hospital as soon as you can to get your scans done so we can see where the cancer is and how to treat it." I said, "OK," and hung up the phone. I looked down at Ava D. and then toward the doorway. I yelled Danielle's name in a strong, deep voice with a mannerism that something was wrong. I looked back down at Ava D.'s tired eyes and then looked up to meet Danielle's tired face in the doorway.

Ten words fell off my lips.

The. Doctor. Called. And. He. Said. The. Cancer. Is. Back . . .

I went in to the hospital for my scans, which showed cancerous lymph nodes along my spine. I was also told that I would need chemotherapy immediately. I was asked to come into Boston on Monday, February 27, for a meeting to explain my options for treatment. It was going to be a total of twelve weeks, with four one-week cycles of treatments at Mass General. I would be full time at the hospital, hooked up to an IV for eight hours a day. Yup! I was going to do the nine-to-fiver, forty hours a week on a drip. That was my new job. I had always envisioned that someday I would be working in Boston in an office that had a great big picture window overlooking the city! But this full-time hospital gig was not part of my plan.

Back on December 16, 2011, when I was lying in my hospital bed, waiting for a room to open in the OR to remove my cancer for the first time, there was a gentleman that I watched walking down the hall as if he didn't have a worry in the world. He was dressed nicely and wore a bow tie. As he walked toward my open door, I bumped Danielle's arm and said, "Danielle, look at that man with the bow tie. Doesn't he look great!" Then I asked her, "Do you think he's a doctor?" She replied, "I have no idea!" Then he turned the corner and was gone. Later that night, that same man came strolling into my room and introduced himself. "Hello, David! I'm Dr. Richard Lee." I glanced over at Danielle, and if her eyes could speak, they would have said, "How's that, huh?" Dr. Lee explained that he was an oncologist and would be taking care of all my surveillance moving forward after surgery. He said I was in good hands for my upcoming surgery, and then he smiled, shook my hand, and walked out of the room.

Now back at the hospital on February 27, waiting in the doctor's office to go over some of my options, the door opened and there was the man with the bow tie, still exuding that look of greatness, with a different bow tie on! Dr. Lee began to explain the ins and outs of the type of chemotherapy I required. I looked right into Dr. Lee's eyes and asked, "How soon could we get started?" Dr. Lee paused for a moment, looked at his computer, looked back at me, and said, "March fifth." As soon as I heard that date roll off his tongue, a crooked smile grew on my face as I stuck my hand out while thinking about the deal I was in the middle of making with Caitlin Moore. I shook Dr. Lee's hand and said, **"OK, Doc, let's do it."**

I stepped outside of the hospital and put a call in to Caitlin Moore. I got lucky and Caitlin answered right away. I began to explain the changes in my life. I started off by thanking her for putting the time into me and also for the invite to California, but unfortunately, I would no longer be able to head to the West Coast for March 5. Instead, I would be checking myself in to a room on the cancer floor the same day at Mass General. Either way, I was still going to be in Boston on March 5!

Now that was a reality check right there. But life is always changing. It's truly out of our control, like the tides, the rising and setting sun, and the seasons. No matter what the change is, there's a beauty in it. *Survivor*, the game, was put on hold. Survivor, real life, was calling my name.

Before I started chemotherapy, my hair was down to my shoulders. I decided to one-up the chemo beast and chop it off before it robbed me of that choice. My best childhood friend, Kylee Kattar, worked as a hairdresser, and she did the honors. Two seven-and-a-half-inch ponytails came off my head and were donated to the Pink Heart Funds. Someone, somewhere, who had already experienced hair loss from chemotherapy, would benefit from a new wig.

After I left the salon, my days became heavily fogged out, thinking of the unknown. I had a hard time focusing on much of anything else besides how to steer myself down this new path to a destination of excellence. Every once in a while, I would think about the question in the newspaper article that read "WILL HE SURVIVE?"

Without fail the day arrived, and I checked into the cancer unit on floor nine of the Lunder Building, at Mass General. I walked into my new office, and there it was: a big wall of windows. I was eye level with the top of Boston's capital building. It had a dome-shaped golden roof that stuck out like a painting, especially when the sun was shining directly on it. My immediate family had all shown up at the hospital along with my childhood friend, Shane Wakeen. There was a vibe of discomfort bouncing off the walls in my room as I waited for my doctors and nurses to get started with my chemotherapy.

I noticed an overhead hoisting device used for lifting patients. The control to this fantastic Hoyer lift was beside my bed and within arm's reach. The label on the machine read "Lifting capacity 400 lbs." I weighed 170 pounds. As I began to hold down the button on the control, the device started lowering a T bar that was about two feet long and about an inch and a half thick. The T bar was attached to a heavy-duty vinyl strap. I could hear Danielle and my mother laughing in the background. Once the T bar got low enough, I pushed the bar up under my thighs so I was sitting on the top of the bar with the vinyl strap between my legs. I held the "up" button, gave myself a little push, and went for a ride. At that moment, **I had the same feeling as if I were up in a tree**. I was free and at peace, swinging back and forth over my hospital bed.

A few minutes later, after I'd lowered myself back down, Dr. Lee came walking into my room to discuss a few things about my treatment. The last thing Dr. Lee said to me before he left my room was "David, chemotherapy does not get easier as time continues. It becomes harder." He also mentioned the number one rule: as an inpatient, I was not allowed to leave the hospital grounds during my weeks of treatment.

The first night that I was hooked up to my IV with chemo flowing through my veins was a long night. My head was full of thoughts about my family, my businesses, and my indefinite flight to the West Coast for *Survivor,* along with many other mixed emotions. The question I was still trying to figure out was, How could I turn a negative into a positive and roll it all into success?

The next morning I stood in front of my big picture windows looking outdoors. The sun was so bright that I could barely see outside due to the strong reflections on the glass from the rays beaming through. The windows became like a rearview mirror. I could see my reflection as I was looking out. Then I noticed the door opening and two nurses slowly walking in as I was still facing the glass. The trip of the drip was that those nurses I was watching in my rearview were actually in the direction I was heading. That was my future. I remember looking at the IV hanging out of my arm and then at my briefcase that was full of work tucked away in the corner of the room. Then I looked back out my window to witness the sun shining off the capital building. There were hundreds of people walking the streets and cars driving all around the city roads. It was the flow of a working world right in front of my eyes with a few small patches of snow left on the ground. I said out loud, with my head pressed against the glass, **"What the hell am I doing in here?"** I thought even deeper about how long this twelve-week drip was actually going to be.

There were now chemicals flowing through my bloodstream, and I had a large window of time allowing my mind to drift completely out of the box. By the middle of the week I decided to pull out my briefcase and thought about trying to get some work done for my upcoming cage fighting event. But I quickly pushed that work off to the side and pulled out a journal. My mother-in-law had given me a light brown leather journal along with a small silver pen. She had handed it to me the morning I left to start chemo. As she passed the journal into my hands, she said, "In case you get bored and feel like writing about your time in the hospital. It might be nice to look back on at some point in your life." I nodded and whispered, "Thank you."

I have always enjoyed weathered books—nice-looking journals with leather bindings or nicely designed hard-covered journals with those colored tassels that you can save your pages with. I never wrote in any of them nor did I read any of the books. But today was a little different. The headline that I wrote in pen at the top of the journal was "I HATE WRITING." Then I closed the journal and put it away. I've always had extremely poor grammar and a difficult time with spelling words. I never found joy in writing or reading due to the lack of practice. What I did find joy in, however, was storytelling. Even more than storytelling was story structure.

I kept floating in and out of a bad attitude. I walked laps around my cancer floor, took elevator rides, walked down to the café, and walked outside the main entrance of Mass General and went as far as the curb. That is where I was asked to stop. I watched crossing guards, police officers, and everyone around me, with my IV pole shadowing every step I took. I was restricted and couldn't help but replay that conversation I had with the casting agent over and over again in my mind. I was pretty stoked about the chance to have my life filmed, edited, and broadcasted in high quality to a widespread audience.

I was ready to show up in California with everything I was made of, right down to the core of who I was. I felt that *Survivor* was the best next step I could take to market myself to the world. **I was after something new; I was ready for change.** I was opening a door that I thought had opportunity on the other side and was ready to explore another unknown world, searching for greatness along the way. I was reaching for a lifestyle that I had imagined as a young child.

In my mind, *Survivor* would be a stepping-stone to get where I wanted to end up. So I was all in! But then I got the call that my cancer was back, and all I could do was count my lucky stars that I had already set myself up for change. I believe in the thrill of committing to something new while learning the hard way by making mistakes, breaking through struggles, overcoming challenges, and paying close attention to options and solutions while striving to create a positive outcome. I believe when one door closes, another always opens.

I thought back to the conversation on the gondola ride back in Jackson Hole, about following yourself around day in and day out filming with a GoPro. With this idea I didn't need *Survivor*—Mass General would become my island. I decided I would now be the casting agent, the director, and the contestant. This would be *Survivor* done my way, while spinning out of control with good, evil, joy, anger, peace, jealousy, love, greed, hope, resentment, humility, inferiority, kindness, lies, empathy, ego, and TRUTH!

Chapter Two

Trip Drip

On Friday, March 9, 2012, the day moved slowly. It was the last day of my first week of chemo. Danielle was on her way into Boston to pick me up, and we would head home for sixteen days before it was back on the trip drip.

I woke up Saturday morning all fucked up! I felt like I had the flu mixed together with a hangover. I was tossing and turning in bed and at times listening to my family downstairs below me. It became uncomfortable for me knowing that I was mentally and physically wiped out and feeling weak. I lay there looking at the ceiling, thinking about Dr. Lee's comment: "David, it doesn't get any easier as time continues. It becomes harder." I finally got out of bed around eleven o'clock, which was late for a lumberjack! I took a shower and looked into the mirror and said, "COME ON!" I tossed on a pair of jeans and a white T-shirt, went into the barn and slid on a pair of boots, and headed outdoors for a walk. Once my body hit the outdoor elements, I felt extremely weak. So weak that I went right back inside and put on a flannel jacket, sunglasses, and a cowboy hat to cover up.

I headed back outside and straight to my pond. It felt like such a long-lost walk, and it had only begun. I had a slow pace walking along an old stone wall, checking out each rock, and moving closer to the pond. The sun was bright, and all the grass around the pond was a yellowish green. The trees in the woods still had no leaves. I had a wild state of mind at that moment for the word *time*. Four days before I started chemotherapy, I was standing in the same spot at the edge of the pond, looking out at a winter wonderland. Eight inches of fresh white powdery snow covered the woods, and there was still a thin covering of ice on the pond. In one week it seemed like it had changed from winter to spring. I truly felt as if the week I'd spent at the hospital shared the same amount of time it takes the season of winter to transition into an early spring.

Shortly after I finished up my walk, it was time for my shot of Neulasta. This was a shot of medicine designed to boost the white blood cell count in my body, which was lowered from the effects of chemotherapy. I was told in the hospital that this was a $6,000 shot without insurance. Lucky for me and Danielle,

Mass General, where Danielle worked, provided great options for health insurance for its employees. We were grateful we had Blue Cross Blue Shield covering all our medical expenses. Within two hours of the shot, my head was spinning, and all my bones and joints became stiff and ached. Three days later I finally shook off the flu-like hangover, and my joints and bones no longer felt sore.

The evening of Tuesday, March 13, I decided to open up my journal that I'd started in the hospital. I stared at the headline on the top of the first page: "I HATE WRITING." I began doing something I disliked. *I was writing!* Then I started to write like a madman. I wrote and wrote and wrote. I wrote in cursive, and when something got intense, I wrote in print, in capitals, and even in lowercase. I was not sure why that happened. I also had no idea if any of the words I was using were spelled correctly, and I had no clue where to put commas and periods. I was moving fast and furious through each page. I stopped at one point and looked back on my writing, and I couldn't even read what I had written. I put my head down and continued to fill thirty-two pages with absolute madness. **On the next page, I wrote out in big capital letters "GOPRO!"**

It was time to break out the GoPro. The small high-tech video camera was going to become my journal. I had so much going on in my mind that I needed something that could handle the speed of my emotions, story-line structure, and ideas moving forward. Pen and paper weren't going to cut it. I figured out a technique that would suit me best. I would carry the GoPro around every day, gathering important verbal and visual content, and at the end of each night, I would pull out the chip and watch myself along with others. I was now able to experience my own behavior in slow motion, rewind it, and watch it again. I would be able to listen to conversations I would have with others and review and dissect each frame as me, myself, and I, along with whoever else the GoPro focused in on. I would observe facial expressions and body language—everything I heard and saw. Then I would label each clip by picking out specific content that would form a story based on real, live "take one" footage.

With this technique of filming and watching the footage, I could go back and write in fine detail about how I saw the world and, more so, back up my written content with visuals. The GoPro was the correct tool for the job. You see, I was still fulfilling that camera frenzy I had about *Survivor.* I was now going to be able to observe my own actions, market myself out to the world under my own control, and most of all, capitalize on an idea that started out as a simple conversation on a gondola ride.

I had a lot of work to do before the big hand would strike midnight at the end of the year. The thrill of the unknown began building inside of me. **Something always happens next in life no matter what, and I was ready to attack whatever was next.**

I didn't book many tree jobs for the two weeks I was home after my first cycle of treatment. On the few jobs that I did book, I knew the guys on the tree crew could handle them alone without me. After they completed all the jobs, they had the option to work in the woodyard processing firewood if they wanted to put in a forty-hour week. I wasn't sure where my head was going to be. I thought it would be best to create two weeks where I could stay away from what a typical day was like in my world, which usually involved being buried in phone calls and making decisions on job sites all day. After that finished up, I would come home and set up in my home office to make more calls and send out faxes and emails to coaches, fighters, and managers to line up fights.

I decided it was time to get busy making a life instead of fading away from my family while trying to make a living! There was an old country song by Clay Walker in which he sang, **"If I could make a living out of loving you, I'd be a millionaire in a week or two."** That was my new mindset moving forward. From here on out, my job was to Love. The newest question was, Who was going to be cutting me a check for my new job? I didn't have that answer yet, but I was going to try to fix that problem in the near future.

Thursday, March 22, was not a typical day for me or for New England. By noontime temperatures hit a record-breaking high of eighty-three degrees. New England's March weather was usually in the forties and low fifties. Danielle and I packed up the girls and headed to the coast.

I think we all may have heard once or twice people say, "Go in the ocean when you're sick because the saltwater cures everything!" I had not yet felt overwhelmingly sick, but I had heard the medical industry use the term "sick" related to cancer, and some family members and friends use it too. So there was no way I was leaving the beach without a good cleanse from "Big Old Blue." As I walked into the ocean with nothing in front of my path but the clear, blue sky and cold, dark blue Atlantic saltwater, I began to fall into a world of my own where I thought, "What if this were my last time in the ocean?" I felt the salt misting onto my face and the water and sand being pulled through my feet as the motion of the ocean shifted continuously with small waves crashing past my knees. I drifted away from this death-related mindset, and I took a deep breath. I threw my hands over my head as I pushed off with my feet and dove forward into thigh-high water. After I was fully submerged, I began swimming as hard as I could. My legs were in a straight position, low to the ocean floor, and my chest was skipping off the smooth, sandy bottom as I glided through the water. My eyes were closed tight, and all I could do at this moment was FEEL!

I can remember going back to a time when someone told me something he believed was important. He started the conversation off by saying, "Don't be stupid in life, OK? I want to show you something important." He picked up a stack of papers in front of him and said, "This is a disability policy." He shook the papers in my direction and began to explain that he felt I did dangerous things in life. He also mentioned that even if I didn't do dangerous things, it was still important and smart to protect myself in case something went wrong. "You never know when, and you may never know why, but something can always happen that you might have no control over. You can only be ready!" he said. Then he explained how important it was to live each day as if certain money didn't exist. He slammed his hand off a desk and began to raise his voice as the look in his eyes changed, as if nobody was even in front of him. He sure as hell wasn't looking at me. He started to shout, "You learn to live without the expense that it takes to provide yourself with a good disability policy. Do you understand me?"

I wasn't convinced. "No, I don't," I said. "I'm a young, healthy guy. Maybe if I was older I would think more about it." Before I could finish my last sentence, he slammed his hand off the desk even harder and screamed, "Don't be stupid so you have a couple extra bucks in your pocket. You do it now while you're young and it's cheap. You swing around in trees all day. You're dangerous every day, and who knows, you could get hit by a bus someday." I was told that insurance may not be enough during a moment of crisis, but at least you will have something taking care of you on a financial level. Then you can always figure out a way to make more money! Money isn't going anywhere, and when you do find a way to make more, protect yourself even more! Then the conversation ended with

"David, you do whatever you think is best."

A few months after that conversation, I bumped into an interesting person at a Business Networking International meeting. Caleb Kirby was the owner of American Family Financial Group. He and I had many conversations during these once-a-week networking meetings. There were also many other people who attended to share whatever they had to offer in their line of expertise. Caleb had offered a variety of different services with his company. The one that caught my attention was a disability policy.

After eight years of filing away paperwork and living a budgeted lifestyle, a light bulb went off in my head and exploded with gratefulness for my father's wise words. When I woke up on Friday, March 23, I headed straight into my home office, pulled open the bottom drawer of a filing cabinet, and slid out a folder that had Farm Family written on the top. On the front page in bold lettering were two words: *sickness* and *disabled*. I was not disabled, but after hearing the medical world and a few others use the word *sick*, I figured it was time to make a phone call. I no longer had to figure out who was going to be cutting me a check for the new line of work I was in!

I had two childhood friends who were on my mind at this moment. It was a matter of time before I would contact them about collaborating on one wild art project, which was taking over my entire world!

That night, after Danielle and I put the girls to sleep, we called up some family and friends. In a few hours, our home was filled with good people, and a bonfire was blazing out back by the pond. If Danielle and I weren't working hard, then we made sure we celebrated with each other or shared the feeling with others. The phrase **"work hard, play harder"** had always been a part of my lifestyle, and that was not something I was about to give up because I was labeled as SICK.

Destruction of property always seems to feel so good, especially when it's your own. On Saturday morning I called up my uncle Peter George to see if he would care to join me for the day. He and I, along with some crowbars, slug hammers, and a couple of saws, destroyed the closed-in front porch by tearing it off my home. I had no real plan or vision on what to do once my porch was torn down. I went into this project with no idea besides knowing that destruction and reconstruction would be symbolic for me. It would become part of my therapy. I would be waking up to work hard on my own property.

The last night home, before I headed back into Boston for another week of chemicals that enhanced the feeling of chemo brain, I stood in the bathroom with a bottle of Gillette shaving cream. I rubbed it all over my head, grabbed a razor, and walked downstairs. I found Danielle curled up on the couch, doing something that I had not seen her do in a long time. Danielle was reading a book. I asked her what she was reading, and she told me it was *The Hunger Games*. Then I asked her what it was about, and after she explained what kind of story it was, I said, "Wow!" Danielle also explained the success of the story. I said to her as I walked out of the room, "That's one fucked-up story, but brilliant." As I started to run the razor across my head, I thought about how nice it would be to have a sit-down with someone with that kind of power with words. I was fired the fuck up that Danielle was reading a story built off of wild survival strategies during this chapter of our own lives.

After I wiped my head clean and dried it with a towel, I looked hard into the mirror at a man who I had never seen or recognized before. A new look can provide a powerful feeling within you. The weather outside was dark with a light, cool rain falling from the sky. I decided to step outdoors for a moment. Once I was outside, I stood there silently and then closed my eyes. Once again, all I could do at that moment was FEEL as the light rain hit my soft, tender, naked scalp.

Monday morning, March 26, came quickly with not much sleep the night before. During breakfast, Ava D. came walking into the kitchen and said, "We made a present for you, Pops!" She handed me a big bright red poster with five different photos of our family glued to it. In the middle of the poster board, in big bold black lettering, it said, "WE LOVE YOU, POPS. STAY STRONG." In between all the photos and lettering were decorations. Ava D. said with a soft, cute, squeaky two-year-old girly voice, "I did all the stickers myself, Pops!"

My mind felt as though it was on a roller coaster ride during the drive into Boston that day. I was coasting toward good moments and twisting through bad ones as I cruised down the freeway. I wasn't even thinking about chemo. The one big thing on my mind was how I told all my workers in the tree industry that it might be a good idea to start looking elsewhere for future work. I did not book any tree jobs during the week I would be spending at Mass General. There was still enough firewood that needed to be processed to keep the boys busy until they figured out their plans. Either way, I made it clear that I was going to be making a move. Whether they decided to make a move before there was no wood left was up to them.

The deep thought I kept twisting into was how to let go of what can be known as the "death grip" in business. This is often difficult to do because you may be scared of letting something that has been a part of your life fade away so you can move on to something new. Who knows . . . it may even be something that could end up larger than life. Moving on might lead to fulfilling something that you once envisioned yourself doing, or better yet, pursuing something that you know you can BECOME. **So I was easing up on my death grip.**

As soon as Danielle and I got up toward the main entrance of the hospital, I asked her to take a photograph with me next to the Massachusetts General Hospital sign, which was dated 1811. I believe all good things come from the 1800s! The best part of the picture was that I was standing in front of the sign like I was at the Grand Canyon or something and wanted to seize the moment. Danielle was standing in front of the sign on the building where she happened to be employed. I never wanted to forget what this place did to me, and it'd only been four weeks total, and I still had eight weeks left to think deep and hard about it. The wild part of seizing this moment was that one person wanted to forget while the other was trying to hold on and remember. The interesting part of two mindsets is when passionate love can hold two strong hearts together during any moment of difference.

Since Danielle and I first started dating, I have tried to get her to play the game of chess. She always said it looked slow and boring. I was hooked up to an IV and had nothing to do for the next five days but pass time. I thought I had the perfect conditions to teach her something she thought was slow and boring, because on the cancer floor, time seemed to move at a pace where it actually felt like life was going backward at certain moments.

Danielle and I were on our third chess game into the night, and she was hooked. Danielle explained how intense she thought the game was. Playing against another person without saying anything at all while being tuned in to your opponent's skill level, trying to predict what they might do next so you can capitalize on what may have been a mistake on their part. I think we all hope for having some kind of strategy for any kind of situation that enters our lives. I think the goal is to try our best at handling each real-life move the best way we can while leaving behind few mistakes. One of the greatest values that we all share is that no matter what problem or challenge we face, it can leave us with a trail of mistakes. Like the game of chess, we all have the power and the knowledge to attack each move made in our own lives in any direction while hopefully learning from what we have done wrong in the past.

The nice thing about each piece on a chessboard is that once the game has finished, all the pieces end up in the same box, like each one of us when it's all over. We are all from the same fucking planet, so shame on anybody if they think they're better than someone else in LIFE! I've always thought a good chess player could play the game by themselves. The trick would be mastering the art of tossing on a different hat as the board turns. The problem I created for myself was that every time my world would turn, my biggest challenge was not which hat to put on, but rather which piece to move because I didn't recognize any of the pieces. There were many pauses in my thoughts about how to even play the game. Or was it even a game? I sat and pondered that question as chemicals continued to flow through my bloodstream.

Since I started chemo, I began to notice something in my parents' behaviors toward one another. Their direct conversations with one another were off. Their body language took a big turn from what my eyes had witnessed my entire life. It was becoming an uncomfortable vibe between the two people who had always inspired me as a couple in love.

I had a lot going on in my own life at this given time. The only thing I could do was acknowledge what I was observing in complete silence and hope that nature would take its course and smooth out the rough path I saw my parents going down.

I had always believed that my mother and father were both strong individuals, and I felt they were tucking away their troubles due to my cancer. Certain people in our lives speak loudly without saying anything at all. I could hear my parents loud and clear every time they were present. I had to stay strong and tuck their troubles away so I could stay focused on my future. Two things I have never had patience for in life are lying and bullshit when it comes to communicating with family. The hardest part of my father's silent behavior was that he had always been one to preach about staying out of the herd and holding on to a wolf mentality. However, every time he was present, he had his face buried into what the majority of the world runs off of today—an iPhone. My father set up a Facebook account and was now part of social media like I had never seen before. It got to a point where he would look up and say "What?" in confusion, as if someone had asked him a question, but no one had even spoken to him. Then he would drop his head back down, tuning out his present life.

It was now four thirty in the afternoon. My IV was unhooked from the saline, and I was waiting for my chemo to show up from the pharmacy. There was talk about how my IV in my right arm did not look so good. There was a lot of fluid in my arm right under where the IV was. It was only day two, so I was hoping I didn't need to get a new IV put in my arm on the second day. I pulled up a chair next to one of my big picture windows and pulled up the shade to let the bright sun shine in on me. I put my sunglasses on and grabbed my harmonica to jam out for a little while as I looked out at the world. I started puffing away on my harmonica with a train-chugging riff, happy as ever. My silver Hohner Special 20 Marine Band harmonica was shining brighter than ever when the sunlight would strike it through my picture window.

The game show *Survivor* had an interesting question in the 114-page packet that was sent my way. The question was "What three nonsurvival items would you like to bring with you to the island?" The harmonica was one of them, along with a pair of sunglasses that I was wearing at the time. The third thing I wrote down was a picture of my family. I had that big red poster full of photos of my family taped up on the cabinet at the end of my bed so I could see it at all times. My life felt on point in the room that I was surviving in at the moment. It was a little different from a remote island, that's for sure, but it was definitely a remote place, that was also for sure!

After my chemo was hooked up, Danielle said she was going to go for a walk to the unit where she worked for a little while to say hello. Once she left, I lay in my bed in a quiet, empty room, staring at my overhead hoisting device. I lowered the T bar down once again so I could throw my legs over it, and I pushed down on the "up" button and started going up. I had the control in one hand and my GoPro in the other. Once I was hoisted all the way to the top, I said, "Look at that, GoPro, upside-down chemotherapy," as I filmed my IV pole with a bag of chemo. I decided to try out the swivel the T bar was attached to. I reached down to touch the corner of my bed and gave myself a good push to get a spin effect going. I shouted out, "Woooooo," creating a good, short-lived head rush and then lowered myself back down to safe grounds.

I had two hours left on the IV, and I was sitting in my bed in a dark room, looking out my window at the city lights. All I could think of was Ava D. and Kiana sound asleep, while I was in a location out of reach to lean into their cribs and give them a kiss and whisper, "Good night, I love you." These nights away from my children had been teaching me to cherish every second of such a young age. I was starting to realize that certain moments were not going to last forever, like being able to scoop them up when they were sound asleep and hold them in my arms to watch them in a moment of rest.

Danielle came bursting back into my room, laughing as she pushed what looked like a computer on wheels. I said, "What is that?" She responded, "It's a Nintendo Wii! I took it from my floor; no one was using it so I asked if I could take it to have some fun with you." Two of my nurses came into my room, following behind Danielle. It was time to unhook my chemo, and I was getting my first bag of saline to start flushing out my system. I still had to be hooked up to my IV for a little longer. The nurses started talking about the Wii in my room and asked in confusion, "Where did you get a Wii?" Danielle explained where it came from, and they thought it was great and wanted to know why the cancer floor didn't have a Wii. It was actually a good question.

Sword fighting on the Wii was completely out of control. We were both whipping the controllers around, cords were flying around everywhere, and most of all, Danielle and I were smiling and laughing, stuck in a hospital room together.

Danielle decided to spend the night at Mass General. She and I fell asleep holding on tight to one another in my hospital bed that night. I can remember being awake for a while, after Danielle was sound asleep in my arms, thinking to myself how lucky I was to have her in my life, and even more so, how lucky I was to be loved by her. Every second of each day, Danielle was full of positive energy at such a challenging time in our lives together, which had allowed me to do the same for her.

Around eleven o'clock the next morning, my hospital room became crowded with a vibe of joy. After leaving early that morning after our sleepover, Danielle had driven back into the city and had brought Ava D. and Kiana with her. My mother and older sister had also made the trip into the city with Danielle for the day. Shortly thereafter, my uncle Mark walked through my hospital door to say hello. Eventually five o'clock in the evening had rolled around, and I could tell that all my visitors were looking a little on the tired side. Everyone gave each other hugs and kisses and said good-bye. I gave my two little angels a big hug and kiss and told them both "Pops will be home soon, and I love you!" My room was empty in a flash, and it was once again me and my IV pole. I looked up at the clock, and it was now 5:50 p.m. My mind was in a good place at that moment because most of my day was spent with my family making the best of what we had, considering the circumstances.

As I was patiently waiting and bored out of my mind for my dinner to arrive, I needed to come up with an idea of something I could do to push myself in a way that would make me feel strong inside. Three days of getting chemo pumped into my body was fine. But I needed to find a way to test myself. What I was really after was something to make me feel sore from the inside out!

I grabbed my GoPro and set it up on my IV pole. I spoke into the camera about what I wanted to accomplish as I listened to the sound of a small machine that was pumping fluids through my entire bloodstream. It was contaminating every thought I had ever thought since I was able to think! For me personally, saying something out loud, writing something down, or doing anything at all a little bit different from only thinking about a good idea had always helped me in life. **It always seemed to mean so much more to actually complete a thought with actions instead of letting bright ideas fade away into a regretful, lonely moment in the future.**

The accomplishment I was craving was to go for a jog! Once I was unhooked from my IV, I would jog down to the first floor and then jog up to the eleventh floor, which was the top floor in the Lunder Building. The goal I was after was to push myself by completing three sessions total, from floors one to eleven by foot, before my head hit the pillow.

While I was still thinking through my plan and waiting patiently for my dinner to arrive, my father walked through my office door. This was a surprise meeting. We sat talking about a few things as I dined on Mass General's grub. My parents had started visiting the hospital on separate days, so I was sure at times it was difficult for my father sitting across from me, knowing that his life was in shambles.

My father saw that I was starting to fade in and out of a light sleep. He walked over to my bedside, gave me a kiss on the forehead, and then drooped his head as he walked out of my office.

It was now 10:39 p.m., and my nurse finally walked into my room and said, "David, you're all done for today!" After disconnecting my IV, my nurse handed me a small cup of water with a few different pills and asked if I was going to bed. I told her I would let her know when I was going to end my night. I was pretty stoked up inside, knowing that my night was only getting started!

I sat up in my bed and took a deep breath, slapping myself in the face about seven or eight times with both hands nice and stiff. It was time to sweat out some toxins. I grabbed my white Reebok Classics, laced them up, and walked out of my office and down the hall with my head held high. I went through the cancer unit's double doors, passed the elevators, and headed straight toward a lit-up red exit sign. **I think it's fair to say that when you're following exit signs in a hospital, you're headed in a positive direction.** So keep going!

I entered the stairwell at floor nine, and I walked up to the eleventh floor. I reached out, touched the sign, and started my jog. Once I got down to the first floor, I banged out a few shadowboxing punches, slapped the number one, and headed right back up the first flight of stairs with some quick feet to get my blood pumping. Once I passed the seventh floor sign, I became winded. I grunted out, "It's all right, I need to keep going." I continued pushing myself until I reached the top. I looked at the number eleven and gave it a side kick and headed down the stairwell of the Lunder Building for my second heat. I was now breathing heavily, forcing me into the present moment of feeling my lungs opening widely and closing tightly. I stopped at the fifth floor and took a deep, painful breath as I looked at myself in the reflection of a window in the door. I gave two thumbs-up as I said loudly, "FEELING GOOD!" As soon as I got to the first floor for the second time, I began breathing extremely hard, heavy, and rapidly, with sweat pouring out of every pore. I took another deep, painful breath while speaking out loud to myself "It's good for the lungs," as I started off back up each step with big, long strides skipping over steps. After quickly passing the second floor, my body began to slow down dramatically with a feeling inside as if my lungs were about to explode. At this moment of exhaustion, I yelled out with little wind in me, "This is good for the heart! Good for the mind!"

As I approached the eighth floor, I yelled out, "MIND OVER MATTER!" Floor nine was my floor, and I was moving slow, grunting out each breath, and pushing hard. My head felt like it was building pressure, my lungs still felt as if they were going to explode, and I was dripping with sweat. I started up the last set of stairs with sweat dripping off the end of my nose, as I growled out, "Need to sweat this chemo out of me. Let it get in, do what it needs to do, and get out!"

The end result for tonight was a success. **I told myself I was going to do something, and I set a goal.** The reward for myself was to feel strong inside, and that feeling was accomplished! I got ready for bed, walked over to the cabinet at the end of my bed, and said good night to my red poster with my family on it. I spoke out loud, "I love you, girls." Then I kissed my hand and pressed it against the picture in the middle of the four of us. I was now ready to lay my head down in peace.

The next morning I woke up to a cloudy, gloomy overcast day. I started the morning off by opening up my supply cabinet and pulling out a plastic bag and tape. I was going to put it over my head and suffocate myself. No—kidding!!!!! It was going to cover up my IV before I took a shower. Usually I would buzz one of my nurses to come to my room to perform this step before I showered, but my room was quiet, and I didn't feel the need to bother any of the nurses. I guess I wanted to be left alone more than anything. I got the shower water running nice and hot and stepped under the shower head. I stood there with both hands above my head and my body pressed up against the shower wall, holding myself up. My head was hanging down low, and my eyes were shut as I listened to the beads of water hit the back of my bald scalp. I felt the water flow and trickle down every inch of my body in complete silence with absolutely no urgency to leave this moment.

Once I was all cleaned up, I tossed on a pair of sweat pants and a T-shirt, and I folded up a red bandana and tied it around my head. Shortly after, two nurses came in and got me back on the trip drip. I made a call to one of my closest childhood friends, Marty Mar. He and I have been tight since we were about five years old. I asked him if he could pack up a backpack full of some tricks and head into Boston later that night to help me out with something.

Danielle made her way back into the city to bring me some lunch. My mother had shown up about the same time with my aunt Mary. Before Danielle left the hospital, she handed me all the mail that had been accumulating for the past few days. There was an envelope from my cousins, the Murrays. This was a great card to get while actually being hooked up to a bag of chemotherapy. The card said in big bold black letters with an exclamation point, "CHEMO SUCKS!" That it did—chemo sucked but life did not! That was exactly why Marty Mar was coming to visit me at Mass General. Once I was released from my IV, he was going to help me find that craving I thrived for—the feeling of being ALIVE and STRONG.

Two hours after my hospital room became quiet and empty, I got a call from Marty Mar. He was on his way to the hospital and only about a half hour out. This ended up being great timing because I had been unhooked from my leash! I was now free. I popped a few pills, tightened up my Reeboks, and headed out the door to meet up with Marty Mar at the elevators.

He stepped out of the elevator with a backpack on ready to go but with a confused look on his face. He wasn't sure what the plan was. I told Marty to follow me as I led us to the healing garden. Once we got to the place I had in mind, I reached out to pull the door open and realized the doors were locked. It was too late, and the garden was closed for the night.

I was kind of taken aback on what I had envisioned at this point, so we now had a change of plans. I said quickly to Marty, "We'll head back from where we came from. We can go to the eleventh floor of the Lunder Building. I was there last night doing some running. It's a good spot because no one is there to bother us." Once we arrived at the eleventh floor, Marty threw his backpack down on the ground, unzipped it, and pulled out a pair of focus mitts along with a pair of bright blue boxing gloves with white palms on them.

I pulled out some medical tape and wrapped up my IV, which was sunken into one of my veins in my left forearm. I did not want the IV bouncing or flopping around during this kind of activity.

It was time to tap into the mindset of a champion. I've been taught that all human beings hold a champion spot deep down within their bones. It's how we were designed. That's the reason we own the top of the food chain. We're all unstoppable with the right attitude. **We all have it in us if we release the animal within.**

After I was all taped up and my hands were inside a pair of boxing gloves, I began working out combinations into the focus mitts, trying to stay loose but break a sweat. It felt great to be in complete silence, hearing the sounds of leather smacking into leather as the boxing gloves connected with the focus mitts in the small concrete hallway echoing with rhythm. I was letting my mind run free, and then Marty started to call out a five count as my punches hit the mitts, keeping me in rhythm. This went on for about seven to eight minutes. I began getting aggressive and throwing hard punches toward Marty's mitts to the point that my shoulders began to hurt, and my lungs started to feel like they did the night before. Sweat started pushing out of my pores. I was beginning to gain that feeling I was craving.

Marty spoke up at one point and said, "Dave, take it easy!" I slowed down and continued working out. After about another minute or so, I stopped to readjust my left boxing glove. I looked down at my wrist, and my eyes almost fell out of my head. I had a huge black-and-blue lump filled with fluid right next to where my IV was inserted in my arm.

Marty looked at me and said, "Dave, I think we better stop." I was trying to stay in a good frame of mind for what I had witnessed. I told Marty that it was an old vein, and I began to laugh.

He said, "Yeah, but Dave, there's a needle in your arm. You better go tell someone; this can't be good!" We packed up the boxing gear and headed back to my hospital room. I called in a nurse to take a look at my IV.

As soon as my nurse walked into the room, I felt like it would be foolish to tell her that I was upstairs on the eleventh floor working out with boxing gloves. I figured it would be best to make up a nice, little white lie and save the truth for another day. Her eyes almost fell out of her head when she saw my arm. She asked, "What happened?" I told her that I had stuck my arm out in the elevator, trying to hold the doors open for someone, and my arm got caught as the elevator doors were closing. Whether it was the truth or not, I had a problem with my arm, vein, and IV.

The nurse called for an IV nurse so it could get switched to my other arm. Both nurses decided to have a doctor come in to take a look. He believed that it was a hematoma. Marty was still hanging out in my room on the couch, and every time I told that same little white lie, I watched him shake his head. After I got a new IV put in, I was in shipshape and ready for more!

The last thing I can remember on Thursday, March 29, was having a conversation with Marty as I was becoming uncontrollably tired. My eyes kept closing as my head fell to the side, and I couldn't seem to stay focused on what we were even talking about. I got woken up in the middle of the night at three thirty to get my blood drawn and vitals checked, and most importantly, I was hooked back up to the start of my last eight-hour drip for the week. When my eyes had first adjusted to the light being turned on so early in the morning, I was in a sense of confusion. I looked at the couch where Marty was sitting during our conversation, and it was empty. Then I looked around my room, still confused about what had happened before I dozed off. I noticed a note on my dry-erase board. There were three large words written across the board: "See you later!"

At 10:46 a.m., I had my nurse come into my room and briefly unhook me from my IV so I could take a shower and get dressed for the day. I finally decided it was time to get some work done for my upcoming cage fighting event, which was only about a month away. I tossed on some black sweat pants and threw on a Combat Zone MMA T-shirt. I figured it would help me get in the zone to organize a few things if I had on the proper apparel. If we look the part, then we are the part! I dug through my briefcase, opened up my laptop, and turned on my cell phone. I sunk into my roll-around, a cushioned hospital chair, and called my nurse into my office to hook me back on the drip. Then it was off to work I went, blasting out emails and texting fighters, coaches, and managers in what I like to call Combat Zone mode!

Danielle showed up late Friday afternoon, leaving behind our two children. She was here to pick me up and bring me home for a sixteen-day break away from the hospital before I had to return for my third cycle of treatment.

At this moment, I am directing my voice as an author to shout out a huge "Thank you to MGH" and to everyone who works in the Pediatric Intensive Care Unit in the Bigelow Building. In the medical world, they have what is called *earn time*. Earn time is something that builds over time throughout the working year at the hospital. It allows the employees to take days off in their position while still collecting a day's pay. Each nurse where Danielle works builds a certain amount of earn time in the course of a working year. I am now taking advantage of interrupting my story to thank each and every person who donated earn time to a woman I love dearly—Danielle R. George! During one intense, complicated chapter in our lives together as one, the generosity from her fellow friends and coworkers allowed her to take time off during the weeks I was admitted. Danielle was able to shift directions as a nurse, and this not only helped her take care of me as one of her patients at Mass General in the cancer unit, but it also created a window of time allowing her to stay focused as a devoted, loving mother to our two children. She was a supporting wife, a friend, and most of all a soul mate during a moment of crisis and difficulty for not only myself but for my loved ones as well.

Danielle and I had a couple of hours to burn off before I was going to be finished with my IV. This ended my second cycle of treatment. She and I decided to go for a walk to the healing garden. The sun was shining bright on the outdoor rooftop garden. I was grateful there was even such a place I could escape to during my time in the hospital. The power of the rooftop healing garden and the kind of energy that trickled through my polluted veins at Mass General is something that I'm not sure I will ever be able to explain. All the trees still had no leaves, there was no new growth coming through on the perennials, and the small patches of grass sections were not yet plush green. I was looking forward to being able to watch the healing garden go into full bloom over the course of my treatment, which was going to stretch straight through spring.

After spending most of my working life outdoors as a lumberjack connected to Mother Nature, with a passion for the changing of each season, the healing garden was where I received most of my treatment. I was able to breathe in fresh air, feel the wind against my skin, listen to the birds chirp, and squint from the power of the rays that the sun delivered into my eyes. I was able to reach out and drag my hand across the bark of a living tree. The garden allowed me to embrace simplicity like when I used to climb around in a tree while falling in love with what the world offered organically.

After Danielle and I returned back to my room and I was unhooked from the drip, I packed up all my belongings and walked out of Mass General with authority. My second cycle of chemotherapy was completed.

Chapter Three

Lifting More Than Your Spirits

On Saturday, March 31, I woke up once again all fucked up! In other words I felt polluted, diluted, mentally disturbed, warped, and burnt out. I had the same flu-like symptoms twisted together with a horrible hangover feeling. I spent the entire day slithering and moping around my home in my bathrobe, trying to understand how something could hold me down the way chemo was pushing on my body. I knew it was only a matter of time before

Danielle would stab me with a needle in the side of my stomach, forcing a $6,000 shot of the good stuff into my system, causing my bones and joints to stiffen up with pain.

The next day was April Fools' Day. Even though I didn't feel well, I made sure I had the shower head turned outward facing Danielle for her first wake-up call. I wrapped a rubber band around the kitchen sink sprayer that faced outward for her second wake-up call. I knew that before Danielle left the house, she usually enjoyed blow-drying and curling her hair. So I made a nice, knotted-up disaster connecting her blow-dryer to her curling iron with the cords to these two beauty tools, to help the flow of her morning move smoothly. I also wanted to make sure she left with an ear-to-ear smile and a slimy hand. So I put a good squirt of shaving cream under the door handle of her car.

Later that morning, Danielle, Ava D., and Kiana were going to be leaving to get some errands done. I was going to have an empty, quiet household for most of the day. While sitting around relaxing and trying to regain strength, I thought uncontrollably about my fast-paced, overloaded, workaholic lifestyle that I had created over the past few years. I drifted into the past and envisioned the wise words that my uncle Mark had once said to me when I was a child. **"David, work will mess up your entire life!"** That phrase was starting to take over every thought that crossed my mind when I contemplated the word *work*.

After sitting in a quiet house thinking all day, I knew exactly what needed to be done so I could shake off what might have been a case of depression. I knew my older sister, Jennifer, had Wednesdays off from work, and Shane Wakeen had a flexible work schedule, and they both loved to hike. I called my sister up to see if she would like to take a drive up to the mountains to go hiking on her day off. Jenni sounded thrilled about the invite, but followed up by asking me if I was going to be OK during something like that. Her concern came from the way I had explained how I was feeling. I told her I was sure I would be fine by Wednesday, and no matter how I was feeling, I needed to push myself to greater heights for inspiration. She ended the call by saying, "Yes, I'm in, sounds great." I heard back from Shane, and he was also available to spend the day with me and my sister.

My uncle Peter called me up shortly after I had made plans to go hiking. As soon as I answered and put the phone to my ear, I heard a low, drawn out "Whaaaat's uuuup?" I responded with "Whaaaat's uuuup?" He responded with another "Whaaaat's uuuup?" Then I busted a gut laughing to start our conversation. He said, "David, what are you doing tomorrow?" I said, "Nothing at all, Unc! Why? What do you have in mind?" He responded, "I have time tomorrow and wanted to know if you felt like working on your porch." I said, "That would be great, let's do it." I thanked my uncle and told him I would see him in the morning.

On Monday morning, April 2, I woke up and put on a new work shirt that Derek Wakeen had designed for Micmac Crane Service while I was in the hospital a week ago. The design Derek created for the Micmac logo was an old, wise-looking Indian head with a quote under it that read, "LIFTING MORE THAN YOUR SPIRITS." Half of the shirt order had white Indian heads, and the other half had black Indian heads.

For some reason, after my first week on the trip drip, I never wanted to put on another Roy's Tree Service shirt again. I didn't want to be a part of holding my head high again for a man who decided to start treating me with no respect. So there was no way in hell I was going to carry his pride along with mine to a destination of excellence. Right then and there I made a life-changing decision: I was going to flush Ricky Roy's twenty-five-year, up-and-running company right down the shitta. Except now it was truly all to be done with no respect. That's right, fuck carrying someone else's name when he's only in it for the ego trip. Or maybe I would finish it off with a slow kill. Either way, time will always show how we decide to put something out of its misery!

After a good, solid eight-hour workday on our home, my day ended out back on a cedar swing, relaxing and watching the sun set between bare oak, ash, maple, birch, beech, pine, and poplar trees. I had noticed that since chemicals had been pumping through my bloodstream, I had not been able to sleep more than three to four hours out of a twenty-four-hour day. So becoming tired became its own battle.

By April 4, I was recharged and as amped up as ever to spend most of my day on the side of a mountain. Jenni and Shane showed up around nine in the morning ready to roll.

As soon as we started our hike, I knew right away that being outdoors, listening to nature, and feeling the cold early-April wind drifting through the leafless trees was what I needed. All the trees had small little buds that were waiting to open up as the warm weather slowly moved into New England. It was an ideal day to clear my mind while creating a strange, salty, stinky chemo sweat. I was a bald, disgusting pig when I sweated going through chemotherapy.

I hit a spot close to the mountaintop where I decided to pick a line to go for a sprint through a large, stretched-out section of ledge and rocks with scattered trees. I wanted to feel my lungs expand and contract and feel my heart pounding inside of my chest.

Once we hit the mountaintop and were above all the trees, and there was nothing more than ledge and rock, it became a moment I will hold on to forever. I stood at the edge of the mountain with the wind tearing at my body as I received the feeling of being free and at peace, standing at the peak of Mount Major. At this moment, **I felt that I was born to win this fight, leaving behind something that may inspire others who are in search of inspiration.**

The next morning I committed to something completely different from standing on the edge of a mountaintop. I would be conducting a day of tree work with two of my workers who were still hanging around looking for work. I woke up nice and early to meet one of my cousins and this twenty-year-old, hard-working, punk-ass kid, Patrick, who always wore an ear-to-ear smile.

When we got to the job site, there were three work trucks already there, which all had the same logos on the door marketing a roofing company. My two workers and I pulled up with our two work trucks—my pickup plus a dump truck and a wood chipper. I noticed that the roofers' trucks were parked right where the tree work was going to happen. Two trucks were in the front lawn and one in the driveway.

I pulled up in confusion about the chaos surrounding the areas where certain trees had to be removed and others pruned, since I had confirmed with the homeowner the day before about my arrival time to start working. I pulled over, put my four-ways on, and jumped out of the dump truck. I made my way over to the house and asked one of the roofers if the homeowner was in. He confirmed that she was home so I gave a knock on the door.

Once she opened the door, we both exchanged good mornings and hellos, and then I asked, "Why did you fail to mention that you were getting your roof reshingled on the day that we agreed to take care of your tree job?" She responded in a bitchy tone. "Well, my husband and I didn't want contractors at our house at different times." But you never know someone's story, so I thought to myself, "Be nice." She then said, "So, please go figure it out with them!" I took a deep breath and smiled and said, "OK, I will go see if they will work with us and move some of the trucks around."

After getting the roofers' cooperation and trucks juggled around, I moved in the chip truck and started setting up in the front yard to begin working. I noticed the lady I spoke with was storming over in my direction. She tossed her hand in the air while saying, "I need to get out of my driveway. You're blocking me in!" As she waved her hand at me a few more times, moving closer to me, I said nothing at all to her for a second. I bit down on my jaw and gave her a stone-cold look with my eyes under my cowboy hat and said, "I will pull out right now so you can get your vehicle out, and then we can pull back in so we can get started on your job." She gave her head a quick shake from side to side and started speaking to me with an angry tone. "I'm not ready to leave yet! I'm not done getting ready!" After another deep breath, I mentioned to her that I would get started on the job if she was going to be a while. If not, I could move the trucks out of the way now. She replied with "I don't know how long I'll be, but when I have to leave, I have to leave right away!"

She made a funny little bounce with her eyebrows and puckered her lips in a strange way. I put my head down to the side as if I was looking at my left shoulder, but I was thinking hard about what my next move was for this lady, who was only two feet away from me in conversation. Then I swung my head right toward her face with direct eye-to-eye contact, almost nose to nose, while both my arms went up and both hands were at ear level, as if I was going to reach out and strangle her skinny little neck. I spoke four deep, loud, direct words to end the bullshit.

"This is poor coordination!"

She said nothing. I then turned to my workers and said, "Pack up the saws and gear. We're out of here." My cousin responded, "We're really leaving, Dave?" I said again, "Let's go! We are leaving; there's no work for us here. If you boys want, you can split firewood to fill your day back at the woodyard, but I'm finished on this job."

Once we got back to the woodyard and parked the equipment, I jumped in my pickup truck and headed home with a smile. I have never acted like that before in the tree industry. I have acted like that many times in other areas of my life but never in the tree industry. As soon as I got home, my cell phone rang, and it was my cousin Melissa. "David, I got a call from a lady. She said you were scheduled to do her job today, showed up, but then left all upset, and she wants to know what happened and if you're coming back. Is everything OK? What do you want me to tell her if I call her back?" I said, "I'm fine, Melissa. I'm not going back to her job. Please don't call her back either; keep her guessing about her tree job and who she called to do the work. Maybe she will even think about her own behavior!"

It was a beautiful, bright sunny day in my backyard, where I knew I could think in peace. I headed over to a bench made out of red oak and hickory wood I had carved up with a chainsaw a few months back. I sat on that bench and took it all in. The sun shined strongly through the scattered clouds. A cool spring breeze blew while I talked out loud to myself about how I was having such a hard time dealing with people who I believed had a bad soul. I guess there is no real, accurate way to tell if someone has a bad soul or what he or she is made of deep down inside, but I think we all have the ability to decide how we feel about certain people after the first impression.

Many of us who go to work or have to deal with other people in our business life might be able to relate to the biting-your-tongue-and-smiling method. As time kept moving forward in my own life, I was losing that mindset quickly toward people who I believed had bad souls or any individuals I had no respect for.

I stayed seated outside on my wooden bench for a while longer, laughing as I thought hard about how I was truly spinning out of control. I even thought about the direction that my behavior and actions were headed in, and how I thought it could make a good TV show called *Dave George and His GoPro: Spinning Out of Control.*

At that moment, I decided to make my next move in my working world by following through with eliminating not only a tree service but a crane service as well, and I also made the decision to hang up my gloves as a cage fighting promoter and matchmaker in the New England area.

On April 6, I woke up tired. I wasn't sure if it was from hiking, chemo, or maybe something to do with making a large, compulsive, life-changing decision the night before. The kind of decision that may affect the lifestyle of not only myself but my loved ones as well. The kind of decision that has a track record of tearing certain relationships apart. I was going to knock out three sources of income to create a window of time to focus on a lifelong American dream. **It was now time for creative thinking, strategic planning, and extreme focus.**

That night, after Danielle and I laughed our way through a family dinner with a five-month-old and a two-year-old at the table, my cell phone rang. I said hello quickly and heard another low, deep, dragged out "Whhhhhaaaaaaaaaaaaaat's uuuuuuuuuuuuuup?" I said back, "Whhhhhhhhaaaaaaaaaaaaaat's uuuuuuuuuuuuuup?" It was my uncle Peter. He asked if I was going to be home tomorrow. I said, "Yes, I am." He responded, "Great! Let's spend some time working on your porch tomorrow; it's going to be nice out."

About an hour later, my cell phone rang again. This time it was a childhood friend of mine, Calvin Kattar. "Dave, what's up? How are you feeling, man?" I replied, "I'm feeling pretty good, Cal! I've been tired here and there but trying to stay focused and strong." Cal said, "What are your plans for Monday? Do you feel like getting in some training?" Calvin had an MMA fight booked for the beginning of November and explained how he was starting his training camp for the fight. I said, "That would be great. What do you have in mind?" He said, "I've been swimming a lot in the a.m. You up for that?" I said, "Hell, yeah. See you on Monday."

On Saturday morning I cranked the stereo in the barn, and my uncle Peter and I put in a good, long, full day fixing up my front porch. The best part of Saturday for me was when daylight was coming to an end, and Ava D. and I were outside playing on her swing set before it was time for bed. I have heard before that moments watching your children in complete joy are absolutely priceless. I am proud to say that I am learning to cherish those riches as I grow.

The next morning I woke up to a special Sunday. It was Easter morning—the celebration of the resurrection of Jesus Christ. I was born into the Christian culture, which celebrates this fine day with church services, festive family meals, and Easter egg hunts for fun. I do not attend church services unless I'm invited to a wedding ceremony or a funeral mass. I believe in God and in myself as strongly as I possibly can every day, without the need to reassure the strong feelings of my belief. There are, however, two beliefs in my life that seem to be even stronger than God and myself:

Miracles and dreams.

Going back to when I was only eight years old, my mother had given me a brass cross. It was eight inches long from top to bottom, four inches wide, and weighed about half a pound. It was my great-grandmother's. I had been told that the woman never missed a Sunday mass. I have only a few memories of her, mostly hugs, kisses, and a wrinkled, loving face.

I guess my mother felt it was something I could hold on to and use to remember my great-grandmother after she passed away. I can remember being told at a young age "Use your prayers wisely." That was something I decided to take seriously and hold a strict rule of discipline toward. I put the cross in the back, right corner of the top drawer of my dresser and let the years pass.

The reason my beliefs became strong in miracles and dreams was because I had experienced two miracles in my short-lived life. The first miracle we named Ava Dorothy George. The second miracle we named Kiana George. Before I left the house to head to the hospital for each one of their births, I reached into the top drawer of my dresser, and without thinking twice, I grabbed my cross and brought it to the hospital while praying as strongly as I possibly could for HEALTH and HAPPINESS for Danielle and our child inside of her. As far as dreams, well, I've been lucky enough that those have been coming true in my life since I've had baby teeth.

Calvin was my wake-up call the next morning, on Monday, April 9. "Dave! I'm going to the gym for eight thirty if you can still make it?" I responded, "You bet, Cal! I'll see you there." I grabbed my Speedo swimming goggles and a backpack filled with my swim trunks, my towel, and most of all my GoPro and headed out the door.

After my second cycle of treatment, I felt run down. Maybe it was the chemo still pushing down hard on my body. I knew right then and there that Dr. Lee's wise phrase, **"It doesn't get any easier as time continues. It becomes harder,"** was lining up wonderfully with the feelings I felt throughout my entire body as time slowly ticked forward.

The best part of the swim with Calvin was when we entered the pool area and there were people everywhere. People were sitting on benches beside the pool; some were watching, and others were resting. There was a full pool with a water aerobics class going on as well.

Some people I could catch staring hard in my direction. Maybe it was because I had no hair on my head or face with thinning eyebrows, and I looked like a cancer patient who had been receiving chemotherapy and was now in a pool area. Or maybe it was the small silver camera strapped to my head. One of Calvin's strongest traits that I have always been a fan of is that he never judges anyone. Calvin is a strong fighter who creates a positive vibe during his company and training. That was what I needed.

My spirit as a fighter was growing stronger as I followed Calvin back and forth. We shared the one open lane at the end of the pool, which was all that was available due to the size of the aerobics class. We completed five sets of twenty-five laps, with all the way down and back counting as one! I felt honored to be working out with an athlete who was training for a big, upcoming mixed martial arts fight, while I was in the middle of my own fight.

Taking the time to spend all morning to exercise my body and mind was important to me. I have memories of hearing all different kinds of people saying the same thing, but in their own words, about parenting, which has always left me wondering.

"Once you have children, it's not about you anymore."

I have always questioned this mindset. What happens if I forget about me? What happens if I stop taking care of myself? What would it be like if I pulled who I was out of the equation? I mean, really, what would happen? I don't have a fucking clue. I've never done it. I do know that I reached hard, lap after lap, knowing that the deeper I dig within, the more I allow myself to love my wife and children correctly. In other words, the fear of forgetting about me, not caring about myself anymore, or pulling who I was out of the equation was propelling me forward, in both the swimming pool and in life.

Calvin and I sat in a hot tub and talked about the fight game as we cooled down from our workout. He and I kept drifting back and forth in conversation about change in our own personal lives. Calvin mentioned he was looking to make a change in his world of organized fighting. We both knew where each other's heads were at and left it at that for now. There was a much bigger prize to keep our eyes on before we spoke any further about business.

My mind was back in Combat Zone mode!

The next two days, I cleared my schedule to drive around. I drove through all different towns, talking on my Bluetooth like a fucking weirdo! I pulled over to the side of the road at every main intersection or stop sign with my hazards on like a happy town worker in a bright red Chevy truck. I was pounding in wooden stakes and stapling poster after poster to each pole, advertising for "Live Cage Fighting." Then when the show is over, the real town workers get to come out and clean up my scattered mess of literature. I worked old school when it came to guerilla marketing. I was taught that if you wanted a job done right, then you had to do it yourself. Plus, I didn't trust anyone involved in the fight game.

On April 11, I was in Combat Zone mode all over again! At midday I stopped at the venue where Combat Zone was going to be held. I was about to walk up a back stairwell when I passed Mike, the head of maintenance at the venue. Mike yelled out, "Dave! What's up?" But before I could even answer him, he said, "You made it on *Survivor*, didn't you?" I laughed and said with a foolish grin, "No, Mike, I did not." He looked at me with a funny look on his face like he had been lied to.

"Ok, I get it, Dave! You can't tell anyone. I've heard of the rules for reality TV before. But you made it, I know you did." I replied, "I didn't make it on the show, Mike." He said, "I know you did,

Dave, but don't worry, I won't tell anyone." I stood there looking Mike straight in the eye without a blink. Mike fired out another sentence that sent me into a world of true enjoyment. He said, "Why did you shave your head?" Before I answered, he fired out another question. "You did it for the show, didn't you?" I smiled without saying anything, until I could feel it in my cheekbones. I finally said, "I'm going through chemotherapy right now. I'm about to head back in to Mass General for my third cycle of treatment in five days. I was not meant to play the game, Mike. I'm living it, man." Mike's eyes looked like they were about to fall out of his face. Then he looked at me and put his hand on my shoulder and said, "David, I'm so sorry." Then he gave me a big hug and said, "It was good to see you; take care of yourself." I looked at Mike, smiled, and said, "Thanks, Mike. I will see you real soon."

I continued up the stairwell to hang up a few more posters throughout the facility, which was going to be filled with over a thousand screaming fight fans in about two weeks.

On April 12, I started a colossal fire at the woodyard and drove around in my front-end loader with Ava D. on my lap, smiling and laughing as we were slowly eliminating some of "Roy's Tree Service" on top of open flames. For the next two days, Danielle and I turned off our cell phones and focused on each other and our two children. Then on April 15, my older sister Jennifer stopped by with Shane Wakeen. They announced they were engaged! My sister was getting married, and one of my best childhood friends was going to become my future brother-in-law.

The next day I checked myself back in to Mass General for the start of my third cycle of treatment. My nurse walked into my room and introduced herself. She explained that I would be needing to go downstairs for x-rays. The nurse also mentioned I had to wait in my room for my transportation to arrive. I responded, "What do you mean 'my transportation'?" She said, "We have someone coming with a wheelchair to bring you down." I looked at her and said, "I feel pretty good; I think I'll walk down." She said, smiling, "I know you probably could, but the transporter wouldn't have a job if you walked down." I had nothing to say back to her response, so I started laughing.

I jumped onto my bed and pulled out a metal jaw harp and started harping away as I waited for my transporter to arrive. There was a knock on my door, and then my nurse poked her head in and said, "David, they are here to bring you down for your x-rays." As I walked out of my room and into the hall, there were two older black gentlemen, who looked as if they were in their sixties or seventies, waiting for me behind a wheelchair.

I sat down in the chair, and one guy started unfolding a thick white blanket and placed it on my lap. I looked up at Danielle's face. She was cracking a bright smile as she watched this unnecessary transportation situation. I looked up at one of the transporters and said, "I can walk down, you know." He looked at me through his glasses and gave me a wrinkled smirk and said, "I wouldn't have a job if you walked down, so sit!"

After my x-rays were completed, I was guided back to the same wheelchair by someone who worked on the floor. I was told to wait once again for my transporter to arrive. I decided to grab ahold of the wheels and roll myself out of the room and into the empty hall. After patiently waiting for about five minutes with no sign of a transporter, I decided it was time to make a move. I knew it was going to lighten up my morning if I traveled back to my room under my own control.

I started rolling down the halls, through double doors, and in and out of elevators. I pushed past a person sitting in front of a computer and started spinning around with a confused look on my face. The person then asked, “Can I help you? You look lost.” I got directions and finally ended up on floor nine in the Lunder Building. I began picking up some good speed while passing by the front desk of the cancer unit. There were two women and one man sitting behind the desk as I passed at a high speed. The man yelled out, “Where are you going?” I continued clipping right along, turned my head quickly, and shouted, “I’M A PATIENT. Room nine thirty-two!” I could hear them all laughing as I rolled on. I made a quick turn and saw room 932 in the distance and beelined it to the finish line. Both of my room doors were wide open, which created a space big enough for me to cruise right in.

I was huffing, puffing, and laughing as I blasted into my room and through a privacy curtain, startling Danielle who was sitting in the corner of the room. She straightened right up and had a deer-in-the-headlights look for a split second. She had two funnels suction cupped to each one of her breasts, pumping out milk for our newborn. Kiana was still on a breast milk-only diet. Danielle was disciplined; she allowed our young to drink only what she produced for the first nine months. She stayed busy using the breast pump between her travels in and out of Boston.

I was laughing my ass off about the whole situation. Once Danielle settled down from my entrance, she asked, “What are you doing? Where are those guys that brought you down?” I replied, “I don’t know! I took off. I didn’t want to wait for my transporter. I wanted to be in control of this chair.” I spun a 360 as my nurse walked in and asked if everything was all right. The front desk told her they saw someone flying by in a wheelchair. I looked over at Danielle's pumping station and saw her shaking her head and smiling as she said, "They're going to kick you out of here!"

I started off the next morning with a set of thirty push-ups. I still had some good strength inside of me and wanted to try to hang on to it as long as I possibly could before my chemo clock started ticking. I knew it was only a matter of time before I would feel physically and mentally worn out. I wasn't quite sure if it was chemo that had anything to do with wearing me out or if it was the speed and quantity of questions and tests that LIFE threw at me as I lived at Mass General for four nights and five days.

By midday I had an interesting meeting in my office with Dr. Richard Lee and Dr. Alicia Morgan. Our conversation was about how I was having trouble with my energy at home without any sleep. I was up all night long with racing thoughts. They didn't understand exactly what I meant. Every time someone asked me "What is the one thing you wish you could improve on?" I had the same answer without even thinking twice for as long as I can remember. "I wish I could better articulate in words what my mind is thinking."

After I remained puzzled and tongue-tied, the two doctors turned to Danielle and asked, "What kind of behavior is he having, Danielle?" Danielle looked right at me before answering and started laughing right in front of both of the doctors, in a respectful way. Danielle said, "I don't really know how to even explain it." Dr. Lee then asked if I was acting compulsive, dangerous, or violent, and then he even asked if I seemed suicidal.

I smiled when I heard *compulsive*. I spoke up and said, "No! It's all good thoughts. The speed of it all is overwhelming. I can't seem to get any sleep. Even after a full day of activity, I can't seem to shut off my body and mind." I asked if chemotherapy had these kinds of side effects or if it could be something in one of the other medications that I was taking. Dr. Lee and Dr. Morgan seemed puzzled after I explained my behavior. They decided to lower the steroids they were giving me. They thought that might help slow down some of my high-speed thinking and lack of sleep. So, at the start of my third cycle, I decided to trick myself. **Whatever Mass General was pumping through my veins was now POWER and STRENGTH!** I began to believe that I was going to become stronger, instead of weaker, as time continued through my treatments.

Later that day out in the healing garden, I noticed there were a few buds that had opened on the trees, but the leaves were still not fully open. New England was slowly starting to transition into spring as Danielle and I sat on a bench outdoors with the sun shining brightly in our direction. I tossed on a light brown Kangol bucket hat to protect the skin on the top of my head. My skin had become extra-sensitive to the sun since the start of chemo, but then again, maybe it was the skin on the top of my naked scalp, since it had been covered with hair since I was an infant.

I was relaxing with my arm around Danielle on a rooftop, looking out at the city of Boston with a clear sight of the bright orange CITGO sign connected to Fenway Park in the distance. Danielle and I gave each other a hug and kiss, and then she headed back home to take care of our children. It was now three thirty, and I was back in my room, pacing around like a wild animal at the zoo that wanted to get back into the wild and be with his family. I sat on my couch for about eight minutes, bouncing my toes, looking to my right and then to my left quickly, back and forth, as if something had changed at the spot where I was looking. I was losing my mind!

I would get up and then lie on my bed as I watched the clock. After about two minutes passed, I would walk into the bathroom, look into the mirror for a second or two and smile real big, and then walk back to the couch to sit or lie in a different position. This act of high-speed, confused behavior went on for about an hour or so.

I walked over to my big picture window, pressed my head against the glass, and started watching the flow of life outside the hospital walls. I grabbed my IV pole and decided to make a trip to the snack room in the cancer unit. As soon as I entered the hospital hallway, my eyes looked in the direction of inspiration heading my way. I saw a girl with a pale, naked scalp with thinning eyebrows like me. I would have guessed she was in her early twenties by the way her face glowed with young, natural beauty. She was on two crutches with one leg in a thick cast that started at her foot and continued up slightly over her knee and ended at the middle of her thigh. She had two nurses by her side and an older lady in front, who was moving a little faster than the group. The lady kept looking back at the young girl as they made their way down the hall. The older lady had the look on her face as if she was beside a loved one every step of the way.

As I continued moving down the hall at about the same pace as the girl moving toward me, I saw that she had a stone-cold look on her face with flames of fire flickering in her eyes as she crutched her way down the hall. The next step, she and I made direct eye contact. It was moments like this where I truly believed I was on a trip drip. I began to drift away into her eyes as if I were walking into a mirror reflecting the pale, naked scalp, the thinning eyebrows, and the same flickering flames in the center of the pupils. As we moved closer to each other while holding eye contact, I slowed down my pace a little bit, and we both turned our heads slightly toward one another and smirked and showed a little glimpse of teeth simultaneously. I turned into the snack room, and she continued down her own path. To this day, I believe that small smirk, which was shared with someone on a cancer floor in a Boston hospital, and with someone I would never ever recognize today if I were sitting across from her at a diner or café, was a true moment of **"the eyes don't lie."** I saw what I saw and took it in for what I wanted it to be. I was inspired and touched forever by a breathtaking moment shared with a complete stranger on my way to get an Italian ice in a snack room.

It was now 4:49 p.m., and I was back in my room and still bouncing around like a wild animal in captivity. I started to bang out some more push-ups to burn off some built-up energy. My goal for a workout plan was to do as many sets of thirty push-ups that I could before my head hit the pillow to help keep myself sane. Shortly after my set of push-ups, Derek Wakeen pushed my door open. I jumped up and said, "Oh shit! I wasn't expecting to see you walk in!" Derek laughed as he came toward me with a solid handshake. "I wanted to surprise you!" Derek handed me a big dark-red book. Once I took it from his hands, I looked down at the cover and read four words in gold lettering—*The Book of Secrets.*

Derek and I chatted for about forty-five minutes on theories and philosophies about life and projects. Derek is not only a childhood friend of mine but also one of the most inspiring, well-rounded artists that I personally know. He is exceptional at creating musical beats and black-and-white sketches. Our conversation mostly got lost on exploring new ideas. I started telling Derek how I was in the process of creating a video journal with my GoPro to help pass time and keep my mind in project mode. I was beginning to know how great it felt to commit to an idea with everything you're made of, right down to the core of each and every bone in your body, to where you actually **become the masterpiece.**

Derek looked at me with a silent, deep-thinking look on his face. Then, as he nodded his head up and down, he said, "That's a real smart idea, Dave." After seeing Derek's reaction and hearing his thoughts on what I had told him, I realized that Derek and I would be collaborating artistically in the near future. Derek and I talked for a little while longer. Then I took a picture of the two of us in my hospital office. I wanted to capture a moment that in my mind was going down in history.

On Wednesday morning, April 18, some of the sun's rays were beaming through the partially open blinds. I pumped out thirty push-ups, jumped in the shower, and washed off what I could of the awful-smelling chemo odor that my body wouldn't stop releasing. As soon as I dried off, I got dressed, and my nurse came into my room and hooked me up to my first bag of hydration, so my IV pole was once again my shadow for the next eight hours. I walked down the hall to the snack room and grabbed myself a grape Popsicle.

There wasn't a cloud in the big city sky today, looking out my window. I had both of my room doors wide open as I sat back on my couch with my feet up, listening and watching the traffic of Mass General's employees, patients, and visitors walk by. Some even rolled by as I waited for my family day to start. I walked over to the elevators in the Lunder Building and pressed my head against the windows and looked out at the city from a different angle than room 932.

I decided to go for an elevator ride down to the main entrance. I walked outdoors to one end of the horseshoe-shaped sidewalk and then to the other side and stood at the edge of the curbing. I spotted a gentleman heading in my direction who I have known since my teenage years. His name was Mr. Joe Santoro. He was the head pharmacist at the hospital. Joe spotted me standing there next to my IV pole, walked over, and said he was on his way to grab some lunch. Then he said, "David, they have really good milk shakes where I am going for lunch. Would you like me to bring back a vanilla or chocolate shake for you?" I said, "Chocolate would be great. Thanks, Joe," and off he went, disappearing into a crowded crosswalk.

I continued wandering around Mass General and found myself getting off the elevator again. My IV pole followed closely behind, and I felt the four small wheels slightly vibrating through the pole that was gripped in my hand. I made my way onto the soft, quiet carpeted hallway on the eighth floor in the Yawkey Building. The vibrating came to a stop, and I no longer heard my feet taking steps down the carpeted hall. Mass General calls the wall in this particular part of their building "the Wall of Hope." The wall was covered with black-and-white framed pictures and stories of all different types of human beings who had hard-fought battles with cancer, as well as with surgeries, radiation, and many varieties of chemotherapy.

The hallway was filled with red, yellow, blue, green, purple, and black-and-white felt flags hanging from the ceiling. They all had handmade arts and crafts on them. As I slowly walked by, the one that stuck out the most had in red lettering "Keep," in green lettering "the," and in blue lettering "faith"!

"Keep the faith."

Being cheered on in life by three words, put together by someone I didn't even know, written on a flag hanging from the ceiling in a hospital hallway, was an uplifting experience. I ended up back outside on the hospital's curbside, waiting to spot Joe on his return from lunch. Sure enough, Joe came strolling on by and made a chocolate milk shake handoff.

I finished my milk shake as I waited in front of an elevator for my family to arrive. Once the chrome-colored double doors opened, I saw Danielle's smiling face as she pushed a stroller out of the elevator with our five-month-old baby girl, Kiana, all wrapped up in a white blanket. Following behind her was Danielle's mother with Kiana's two-and-a-half-year-old big sister, Ava D. Ava was wearing a pair of white sandals, tight white capri pants that had ruffles on them from her knees down, a khaki spring coat all buttoned up, and a purple bow in her hair. I couldn't take my eyes off her as she continued walking slowing toward me. As I reached down with both arms, she opened her arms up at the same time. I picked her up and gave her a kiss on her smooth, soft little cheek.

I said right away, "Let's all go to the healing garden; it's gorgeous outside." Ava D. smiled a huge smile and then sunk her head into her khaki coat as she looked at me in an unfamiliar kind of way. As we walked to the garden, I watched her eye my IV pole up and down, and then she focused for a few seconds on the machine that was actually pumping the fluids into me. Then I watched her follow the clear rubber hose from the machine into the side of my arm. We stopped at what is called "the Touch Stones" before entering the healing garden. Ava D.'s eyes lit up when she saw the big bucket of stones. The bucket was the perfect height for her to walk over and dig her little hands into the smooth stones all by herself. She looked back as she approached the stones with a look on her face as if she was asking permission to touch. I gave her a smiling yes nod, and she began searching for a stone.

Kiana was lying down in her car-seat stroller as I reached over and peeled the shade cover away so I could look down at her. As I was doing this, she picked her head up to look around for a quick second or two. The sun was shining on her baby face, and she had a gums-only smile as her eyes squinted. I looked over at Danielle sitting with her arms wrapped around Ava D., rocking back and forth as their hair blew around in the wind while giggling and laughing.

I asked Danielle's mother if she could take a picture of all of us outside in the healing garden. The four of us sat on a large rock, and behind us was a mature-sized Japanese maple tree that was almost in complete bloom. I had my left arm around Danielle with my hand on her shoulder. Kiana was in Danielle's arms at this point, and she was wearing a light pink golf shirt with her collar popped, tight white capri pants like her big sister, and no socks on as her little baby toes wiggled in the wind. Ava D. was sitting on my right knee with my right arm wrapped around her, and of course my IV pole, or "shadow on wheels," was right beside us for a family snapshot. I was holding in my two arms everything that mattered the most in my life, with a massive smile, as my mother-in-law seized the moment!

Tonight was date night for me and Danielle, and we'd be seeing some family and friends too. I needed to go beyond Mass General's curbside! I am a firm believer that most rules have been designed to bend, stretch, and even twist in life.

My sister Jenni, my friends Shane, Calvin, and Kylee, and another good friend of mine, Jose Madera, were all going out for some Thai food. Jose is the head coach and owner of Intense MMA and the 978 Boxing Club in Lawrence, Massachusetts. Jose has become a close friend of mine over the years in the fight game.

I threw on a black Combat Zone MMA zip-up hoodie and walked out of my room. I happened to pass by the nurse who was taking care of me. She asked where I was going, and I responded that I would be back in a while. I continued on my way, following exit sign after exit sign. Crosswalk after crosswalk, I walked through Boston without a care in the world except for the car that laid on its horn and almost drove into me. I think the person in the automobile was pissed off because I was lagging behind, filming everybody with my GoPro and not paying attention to oncoming traffic.

After a few more crosswalks, we were in front of the restaurant Cuisine of Thailand, The King and I, for some fine dining. I saw a few people hanging up their jackets. I looked at Danielle and said, "It would be best to keep my hoodie on, right?" She smiled at me and said, "Yes, keep it on. I don't think you need to be sitting at a restaurant table with a taped-up IV hanging out of your forearm."

Kylee will always have her own memory of dining at The King and I. She ordered a garlic shrimp dish. As the waitress leaned over the table, the plate tipped, and Kylee ended up with a shrimpy, garlicky, brown sauce pouring down the middle of her breasts, filling up the front of her white T-shirt.

It's always funny to watch someone else get food dumped on them at a restaurant. It's even funnier when the person that it happened to laughs along with the party. We finished up our fine dining and headed back to Mass General.

Later that evening I was sitting on my medical bed when I looked up at the clock to see it was eleven. I still had so much energy after having such a good night out with everyone. Plus, I had told myself earlier in the day that I was going to head up to the eleventh floor where it was quiet to get in a workout before my head hit my pillow ending the night. I really wanted to stick to my word and push myself to create a good sweat and wear myself out to a point where I felt like I could collapse.

Danielle unfolded the hospital couch into a bed and laid out a few sheets and a pillow. I jumped up off my bed, walked over to Danielle, and gave her a kiss goodnight. Then I walked over to a bag in the corner of my room, unzipped a small section on the side, and pulled out a jump rope. Jump roping was one of my favorite exercises to break a sweat. I walked out of my room wearing a tight blue tank top, black sweat pants, and laced-up Reeboks, with my jump rope wrapped around my right hand. I saw my nurse sitting quietly at a computer in the hall. I felt like it would have been rude to pass by her and say nothing after she looked up and noticed I was looking at her. I said, "Hello!" She said hello back and asked, "Do you need something?" I answered, "No, I'm all set. I'm going for another walk; I will be back soon."

The sound of turning the door handle on the eleventh floor sounded like freedom. The quiet, empty hallway with dim yellowish lighting was truly a spot where I could forget about the word *patient.* I started off by holding the jump rope handles in both hands and swinging the rope around both sides of my head until I had a comfortable rhythm going. I began slowly trancing out mentally into a quick, steady pace of jumping rope. My lungs got tired, my pores pushed out sweat, my head built up pressure, and I felt nauseous at times—all common symptoms in the moment of working out the human body. After about seven to eight minutes of good, strong, focused jump roping, my toes came in contact with the rope and I was interrupted. I put my head down and started taking some deep breaths. Then I raised both arms above my head with the rope stretched out in both hands while leaning up against the wall.

It was amazing how much inner energy chemotherapy was sucking out of me. Even more amazing was how much my body and mind would crave the feeling of suffering to create a stronger mindset as I pushed through each day.

I paced around for a few more seconds, and then I looked into the GoPro and started speaking to it as if there were an audience. I gave a thumbs-up with my right hand and said, **"This last session is what's going to make you sleep good. Keep your head straight. POSITIVE THINKING!"**

I began swinging the rope around my head again, creating a new rhythm. After about five minutes, I hit a point where the feeling of collapsing was creeping up on me. I decided to slow my pace for a cooldown. That only lasted about twenty to thirty seconds, until the rope came around one last time and hit my toe, ending whatever rhythm I had left. I closed my eyes and grunted out a deep breath from my gut and let my body fall to my left into a wall. As soon as my hands hit the wall, I dropped my jump rope, and the only rhythm I had going was quick, heavy breathing as I rubbed my midsection, trying to comfort my lungs.

I picked up my jump rope, draped it over the back of my neck, and walked up to the GoPro as if I still had an audience. I gave two thumbs-up with a smile!

The next morning, I woke up at eight o'clock to Danielle cracking the blinds in the room to let some sunshine wake the both of us up. She was rushing to get back home to Ava D. and Kiana due to Kiana running low on breast milk. Danielle leaned over the edge of my hospital bed, gave me a kiss on my tired, worn-out face, and said, "I love you so much! I will call you later." Then she rushed out of my room to get back to our little girls who needed their mommy as much as she needed them.

One of my nurses came into my room and unhooked my IV from my last bag of hydration. She announced, "David, it is time to start your first bag of chemotherapy." Once she cleaned out my IV, she attempted to get a blood return to see if the IV was still working properly. She looked up at me and said, "This IV doesn't look good, David." She started tapping the bottom side of my forearm. It looked and felt as if she were tapping the bottom of a water balloon. After a few more twists and turns on my left arm, she spoke up and said, "David, I don't think it's going to be safe to put an IV into this arm." I looked at her and said, "Okay. Do what you gotta do." She started feeling around on my right arm and made a comment about the lower part of my arm near my wrist. "What happened down here?" she asked. I told her about how I had a hematoma going back a few weeks, along with the elevator story!

She said that most of the veins in my right arm looked pretty worn and used. She kept feeling all around my arm, rubbing different veins as her fingers glided over my skin. She stopped on a spot that was on the inner-bottom side of my forearm where the elbow bends. "That looks like the best place, David. I know it's not in a comfortable spot, but the vein looks good. Are you OK with this spot?" I didn't care where she stuck that IV; I wanted to get hooked up again so I could continue with my treatment and move closer to completion of my third cycle of chemotherapy. I said three words to my nurse: "Let's do it!"

I was becoming part of my hospital bed today. Every time someone would poke his or her head into my room to ask if I needed something, I would turn my head toward the door and slowly open my heavy, drained eyes and say, "I'm all set, thank you." I finally opened up my eyes and saw that the clock read two thirty in the afternoon. I was pushing fourteen and a half hours sunken into my hospital bed. It seemed like the only thing dripping into my IV hose today was sleeping medicine. I couldn't seem to snap out of lazy mode.

The next nurse who walked into my room came in with lots of spirit and a pep in her step as she walked over to the blinds and said in a strong, direct voice, "Come on, David. It's time to get up and move around!" She pulled open the blinds all the way, and the sunshine destroyed my lazy mode.

I finally made it into the bathroom. I showered, scrubbed my tusks, looked deep into the mirror, had a quick conversation with myself, got dressed, and then turned my cell phone on and noticed a high volume of messages and missed calls. Then I decided to stroll down to the cafeteria to fill my empty stomach before I took care of some business calls.

My hospital room was still a constant office with my cell phone at times. I pulled out a note pad and pen and started listening to my voice mails. Most of the messages were related to Combat Zone MMA because the show was only eight days away. The month before fight night, my head would normally be attached to a mobile phone. Since I have been promoting live cage fighting, I got pretty good at receiving bad news. I learned to wake up every day with the mindset that 75 percent or more of people in this particular industry wouldn't follow through with what they said they were going to do.

There was one particular voice message that sent me for a spin. I had no patience for people who were straight-out fucking stupid and rude and demanding. The voice mail was a worked-up male. His concern was about a tree job that was done back in early March. I had gone and done the estimate myself and spoke with the homeowner right before I went in for my first cycle of chemotherapy. The job was written up on a Roy's Tree Service estimate slip. Four large red oak trees were to be removed with a full cleanup of all the logs and brush. The crane, chip truck, brush chipper, and log truck would be on site along with four workers. At the bottom of the slip, with a star next to the work order, it read: "*Stump grinding NOT included." Under that was a spot for the total cost of the job, which was $2,800. I tore off the top copy of the slip and handed the written-out job description to the homeowner. I kept the other two carbon copies—one for myself and one for the office. I also explained that I was in between chemotherapy treatments, and if he would like me on the job, it would have to fall on a certain week that I would be home from treatment. Or I could line up the work to be completed without me on site.

The homeowner called back and spoke to Melissa and told her he would like to schedule his job as soon as possible. I put together a crew to take care of the tree work while I was in Boston getting my first cycle of treatment at Mass General.

The upset gentleman said on my voice mail, "David, I have tried to get in touch with you for a couple of days, and I don't appreciate you not getting back to me! I want to know when you are coming back to take care of my stumps like you said you were going to do when you were here pricing out my job. The trees are all gone, and your guys did a great job cleaning up, but no one has taken care of my stumps. I gave one of the workers a check for twenty-eight hundred dollars, and I expect my stumps to be taken care of. Stop ignoring me and call me back!"

This was all said with a direct, frustrated tone of voice, and I played the message again to reassure myself that I was not going crazy or having a bad attitude about customers. I wrote his number down on my note pad and then dialed. After a few rings I heard, "Hello?" I responded with "Hello, this is David George." He interrupted, "Oh yeah, thanks for finally getting back to me! This is how you run a business? You take people's money and don't get back to them?" I said nothing and let the angry customer continue. "I have paid my twenty-eight hundred dollars, and I want someone to come back and take care of my stumps like you said you would after the trees were down!"

I took a deep breath and then smiled real big as I let my breath out and said, "Sir, I am getting back to you right now. You called my phone twice on Tuesday, once on Wednesday, and then called the office, and the secretary told you she would pass along the message. My apology on a delayed callback to your emergency. I have been at Massachusetts General Hospital receiving my third cycle of chemotherapy. In all honesty, I was in no rush to call you back, and yes, we have collected your twenty-eight hundred dollars." My voice began to rise as I said to the angry customer, "As far as your stumps go, well, they can go FUCK their mother!" Then I hung up the phone.

A little later that night after dinner, Jeff McGurren stuck his head into my office and yelled, "Yooooo!" I turned toward the door, jumped up off the couch, and told Jeff, "Come on in!" This was the first time I had seen Jeff since starting chemotherapy. He looked at me and started laughing as he said, "Look at you!" I began explaining to Jeff how I was in the process of creating a video journal with my GoPro.

Jeff McGurren had branded a company using two words: "Articulate Creation." One thing that has always been inspiring to me about Jeff was his ability to edit and intertwine musical beats to flow with video footage in a unique, artistic way.

What opened my eyes most about Jeff's artistic talent was when Caitlin Moore sent a compliment in Jeff's direction before hanging up on one of our phone calls during the whole *Survivor* interview process. Caitlin said, "David, I want to let you know that the casting video you sent in was the best edited video that *Survivor* and I have ever seen. I have been working with *Survivor* for over a decade." In one of our first conversations, Caitlin explained to me that the game show received about twenty-five to thirty thousand casting videos each season. The game show was getting ready for its twenty-fifth and twenty-sixth seasons. It brought me to a new level of appreciation for Jeff's talent in the craft of video editing.

Jeff is the kind of person who drifts outside the box when it comes to new ideas about what might be next in the world of projects. Jeff and I spoke for a little while longer, and my adrenaline started to build. I had my own wild visions during our conversation that I wasn't even able to explain or discuss with Jeff at the time. I gained a lot of confidence as we continued speaking, knowing Jeff and I would be collaborating artistically in the near future.

On Friday, April 20, I woke up nice and early feeling great, knowing that I only had eight hours left before I headed north for another sixteen-day break from the trip drip! My nurse informed me that if I drank enough water, I could skip my second bag of hydration, which meant I could shave off about an hour of being hooked up to my IV. Danielle came through the door at seven that morning with Kiana in her stroller, ready to help pack up my belongings and get back to our homestead.

I took Kiana out of the stroller before packing it to the top, leaving no room for baby Kiana to go back in. Danielle strapped on the Baby Bjorn carrier, and the three of us busted through the double doors with the cancer unit sign at our backs, heading straight for the elevators. We went beyond Mass General's curbside, crossed the crosswalk, entered the parking garage, started up Danielle's Acura, reversed out of the parking spot, and headed in one direction . . . FORWARD!

Chapter Four

Top of the Food Chain

The next morning, Saturday, April 21, I woke up polluted, diluted, mentally disturbed, warped, and burnt out. On this particular morning, my thoughts were overpowering any kind of flu-like hangover feelings I had ever faced. Sleep was not an issue, but I still didn't pull myself out of bed until the clock started counting away into the afternoon hours.

I came home to enjoy my family, but I couldn't even enjoy

myself at the moment because I was tossing and turning under my sheets. Around two that afternoon, I made it down the stairs, holding a pillow in my hand, and climbed onto the couch for more rest. Ava D. was running around our home in her own two-year-old world, laughing and playing, full of energy, as I sunk deeper into our couch, feeling like a failure. This feeling intensified when Ava D. came running up to me, stopping with her nose about seven inches away from mine and looking right at me, saying, "Pops, play with me!" I gently answered, "Sweetie, Pops can't play with you right now." I wasn't sure if I felt like a failure because I was acting like a couch potato or because I had started off a sentence with "can't" to my two-year-old daughter.

Then I heard Danielle's voice calling my name from the next room. "David, come over here. I need to stick you with your Neulasta shot before it gets too late." I took a deep breath and slowly got up, knowing that I was hours away from topping off my fucked-up mindset with aching bones and stiff joints. Having the flu or a bad hangover with sore bones and joints was bearable to me. The issue was how I was choosing to handle my thoughts. I spent the rest of the day dragging my pillow up and down the stairs from the couch to the bedroom. Within a few hours of my Neulasta shot, my bones and joints seemed fine, but my chest became extremely tight and breathing was not comfortable.

I woke up the next morning even more fucked up in the head than the day before, to the point where it hurt to even write about it. I rolled around under my sheets and let the clock tick into late morning. Danielle was downstairs with Ava D. and Kiana. I could hear my family playing below me in the family room as I pulled the covers over my face, still trying to shake off this unfamiliar feeling that was building throughout my entire body. Every once in a while, I would hear Ava D.'s little feet run up the stairs and stop at the top of the staircase. Then she'd start shaking the child-proof gate as she yelled out, "POPS!" Then I would hear Danielle run up the stairs and say, "Ava, Pops doesn't feel good; he needs to rest, OK?"

My heart would shatter every time I heard Ava D.'s little feet run up the stairs to shake the gate, knowing that I was in no condition to go downstairs and play with my child. Once again, I heard little feet walking up the stairs, quietly this time. I heard her hands grab ahold of the gate. Then it got silent. Ava D. was standing quietly at the top of the stairs; maybe she was drifting into thoughts about why her pops was behaving this way. Whatever it was she was thinking about, she started aggressively shaking the gate to a point where it didn't even sound like a two-year-old had ahold of it. She started crying and yelling out, "Pops . . . Pops . . . POPPPPPPS!" I heard Danielle's feet run up the stairs to pull Ava D. off the gate. Ava D. started crying loudly as Danielle carried her down the stairs. Tears began running down the sides of my face as the sound of her crying voice faded away.

My head felt like it was going to blow off the top of my body as I heard her little voice in tears as she was being carried away by her mother because of my condition. **I couldn't even understand who I was,** never mind my family trying to figure out what was happening to me. What I did know was that I was not even mentally or physically capable of playing with my family, and it created flowing tears down my face with a confused feeling as a storm of thoughts progressed in my mind.

I was facing a deep-down battle within myself at this moment in my life as I lay in my bed, not so sure if I was proud of who I even was! I wasn't quite sure if I was having a hard time this weekend with the flu-like hangover feelings or if it was the tightness and discomfort in my chest as I inhaled each breath of air. I even started to think crazy thoughts like maybe I was becoming a bad husband and a terrible father. Maybe I'd even caused these thoughts by making compulsive decisions on starting the process of eliminating what I did in life that generated money to provide a lifestyle that Danielle and I had grown accustomed to and were now sharing with our children.

I knew there would be sacrifice headed fiercely in my direction as I pursued my lifelong dream. With this dream would come full-time selfishness and neglect toward not only myself but my family and friends. And, most of all, **the three most important girls in my life** were about to be blindsided by my actions without any real explanation.

I would drift into thoughts, questioning if I was all fucked up from lying in a hospital bed in an operating room at Mass General four months ago and having a doctor chop off my right nut. Or could the mindfuck have come from the invite to California for a shot at the game show *Survivor* two months ago, and instead of booking a flight out there on March 5, I moved into Boston's Mass General to start my drip of chemotherapy on the same exact date. At times I even thought about how my mother and father's relationship was being torn apart in a hurtful, dishonest, and disrespectful way after they chose to love and honor one another all these years. Their actions seemed to have an impact on my thought process as time continued.

After seven weeks of restless sleep, I thought maybe I was becoming delirious about life, or maybe my actions were caused by the chemicals that had been flowing through my entire body for the past seven weeks. Or maybe my behavior was right on point, all results normal, and whatever I was feeling was real and I was awake!

By acting this crazy in my thoughts, I actually felt great deep down inside to be that far gone mentally in such a wild, distracting, yet angry way. I was nervous to let this kind of energy build up inside of me because I feared what could happen if I bumped into someone who I was not a fan of. I became scared for the way my life could turn out in the long run due to the unstable behavior I was capable of releasing upon either myself or someone else. I fought off the crazy thoughts in the comfort of my own home with the mental strength that we as humans all share deep down inside.

I knew for sure that I was not alone in the world when it came to living through difficulties involving certain mindsets. So, on April 22, I pushed through my own difficulties like I have never done before. I told myself that no matter how intense or crazy I may feel, there is always an ending. The next day I got out of bed at three thirty in the afternoon with the same mindset as yesterday—all fucked up! But it was time to snap out of this poor-me attitude and get focused on something that would inspire my thought process. It was time to GO OUTDOORS.

I pulled myself together, got up and took a shower, threw on some briefs and white socks, and put on a pair of gray parachute pants while tucking the bottoms into my socks. I tossed on a black long-sleeved T-shirt and capped my head with an old faded-out dark blue Mecca bucket hat that I've had since 1999. I strapped the GoPro to my head and was ready to feel the fresh air.

I tossed a mountain bike into the back of my truck. Then I threw on a dark hunter-green Cabela's Gore-Tex rain jacket and drove to a conservation area in New Hampshire, not far from our home. This land had acres of old stone walls built back in the

1700–1800s with wide open fields surrounded by a large variety of trees, shrubs, and weeds. There were also large ledge rocks in areas with high views, as well as low views with streams crossing through the fields. The best part of this land was that there were many places you could end up where you didn't even hear cars driving by. What made this day so nice was it was raining, and there wasn't another car in the parking lot, which meant it was going to be extra-quiet on the trails through the woods.

I got on my bike and pedaled as hard as I could through the woods, creating a good sweat. One of my main goals was to sweat out as much chemo as humanly possible before I headed back to Mass General. I stopped at a quiet spot deep in the woods, jumped off the bike, and placed it up against a tree. I hopped up on a large rock and paused in a squatting position on the ledge as I looked around, scanning the woods and listening to the rain lightly tapping on the leaves above me. I took my bucket hat off so I could feel the cool rain on my bald head.

I got on my bike again, and I could feel that I was slowly becoming proud of who I was again as I biked my way through the outdoors, creating a solid workout that made my heart pump good and hard. As I came pedaling uphill, I entered a vibrant green grassland. The rain let off as the gray clouds in the sky broke up in all directions, allowing spots of bright blue to slowly take over the entire sky. **I held my thumb up high to the sky and felt complete after a good two hours playing in Mother Nature.** My own attitude changed at the same pace as the weather as it transitioned from a dark, gloomy gray day of rain into a clear bright blue afternoon of sunshine.

Once I returned home, I changed out of my wet clothes. I threw on a pair of old, traditional black karate pants, tossed on a skin-tight gray long-sleeved thermal, and slid on a pair of black sandals. Then I made my way up a skinny stairwell that led to a workout room in my barn.

The whole room, including the ceiling, walls, and floor, was painted a light gray. I had two old large sets of 20-ounce red boxing gloves hanging from the ceiling. These gloves were worn by me and my father working out in our basement. I can remember throwing these gloves on and going at it with my old man from the time I was six years old, and the gloves were almost bigger than me at the time. This kind of sparring went on with the same gloves up until I was around fourteen years old. My father would always end our workout session by delivering a shot into my face or my gut, sending me to the ground. The memory I still hold with me today from our workouts is when I finally could get up and look him straight in the eye. He would be laughing with a father's love, and we would either tap gloves or hug before we called it a night.

There was also an American flag pinned up on the ceiling above an incline dumbbell bench. I had two heavy bags hanging on the same beam about ten feet apart from one another. One was an old white cloth bag all taped up with red duct tape to hold its shape and hung low for leg kicks and midsection kicks. The other was a blue canvas heavy bag. This bag was hung up higher and wrapped up with gray duct tape and black electric tape on some parts of the bag to separate striking spots. I had a speed bag set up right above a window in the training room. I had a mirror on one wall for shadow boxing and to practice using correct form. There were signs and posters all over the room that I had collected over the years from previous Combat Zone MMA shows for inspiration when I entered what I called "the fight room."

I put on some of Derek Wakeen's music that I knew would take me on a journey and free my mind, in a spiritual kind of way, as I began a heavy bag workout I used to do with one of my old coaches during Kali classes.

It was a good hand-eye coordination drill that flowed with rhythm to create a great upper-body burn. I grabbed a black leather sheath that was hanging on a nail and pulled out two wooden sticks that were each three feet long by about an inch and a half in diameter with burnt tribal markings going down the sides of each stick. I tapped the wooden scrimmage sticks together three times and began my workout. I was losing full control of my thoughts as the music continued, and my arms became weightless as the burn intensified throughout the long track of trancing beats. I held a seven count on striking the heavy bag while staying as light as I could on my feet. I had no mind at this point and was healing myself in a colorful, healthy way that was strengthening who I was deep down inside with a simple martial art form in a section of an old barn. I played Derek's same beat over and over again until I was soaked in chemo sweat, leaving my body, mind, and heart drained of everything negative I had built up inside of me the last two days.

The next morning I woke up to a shitload of missed calls and an overload of texts on my cell phone, all concerning Combat Zone MMA. The word on the street was that I had canceled my show because I had CANCER. So I guess it would be fair to say that I was diagnosed as being useless by some spineless punk out on the streets in the fight game. I guess his mindset was that me having cancer meant I was unable to organize live cage fighting. The one thing that will always be out of our control in life is what another person might say. I believe the only way to handle that kind of situation is to stay strong as an individual and to knock down the weak with actions by completing something you said you were going to do, never mind what kind of talk is floating around in the air!

I sat down at my desk and pulled out an envelope that had "Combat Zone MMA 41" written on the tab in blue pen, and I started calling back all the important people that actually had a hand in making the show happen. Most of all, I got in touch with the fighters, coaches, and managers to clear up the false rumor going around the local MMA scene.

I had everything in place, and the show was going to happen whether I was dead or alive at this point. The only thing that had to happen was all the fighters had to show up on Thursday at Rockingham Park for six o'clock so the New Hampshire Boxing and Wrestling Commission could weigh in and clear each fighter that was competing on Friday. After clearing up all the bullshit from the morning, there was no doubt in my mind that "Friday Night Fights at the Rock" wouldn't go down without adrenaline trickling out of the cage. It would be a night filled with entertainment, keeping fight fans wanting more after the last competitor's hand was raised to celebrate victory!

After I patched up Combat Zone, I shut my phone off. It was time to play with my children. We started off with a game of "chase Ava D. around our home." Kiana started the chase with the guidance of both my hands under her midsection, holding her out far enough so it looked like she was flying, after I strapped the GoPro to my head and started rolling. Real life, take one! Kiana had on a little white onesie with tiny colorful polka dots on it. Once Kiana was in flight, Ava D. took off running with Kiana tailing right behind her. Ava D. was wearing a multicolored striped hooded sweat shirt and a pair of black fleece pants with white socks.

Ava D. was laughing hysterically as her little feet dashed down through the kitchen toward our back hall. The door was closed to the back hall, and Ava D. never slowed down as she approached the door. Once she hit the brakes, her left fleece pant leg got caught under her foot, and she went crumbling into the corner of the wall and into the closed door at high speed. It took the laugh right out of her so fast and left her lying on her back on the floor looking up at me and Kiana. I reached down and gave Ava D. a helping hand back to her feet, and the chase continued.

Thursday, April 26, was the morning of Combat Zone's fighter weigh-ins. I got up nice and early and headed down to the event room to start assembling tables and chairs. The New Hampshire Boxing and Wrestling Commission would arrive later that evening to clear each fighter who was scheduled to fight under the lights tomorrow night. I was also setting up a twenty-four-foot, six-sided cage that the fighters would all duke it out in. Every piece of the Throw-Down Cage I was building had red-and-white confiscated DEA stickers on them. I had purchased the cage off a local police department after a drug bust a few years back.

While setting up the cage, I received a call that delivered bad news. I found out that my luck had run dry in the world of dollar-bill lending. For the first time I had a deal that went sour; I was fourteen thousand dollars in the hole. I stood there with a look on my face like I had the wind knocked out of me.

The cage was almost assembled, so I walked off to the bathroom, and one of the helpers that I had hired quickly jogged over to me and asked, "Dave! Are you OK?" I stared him right in the eye and said nothing. Then I leaned in and reached out my neck so my face was nose to nose with his. I bit down on my back teeth and said out loud in a strong, direct voice, "No! No, I am not OK. I'm actually on fucking edge at the moment." Then I asked him to please get back to work as I walked away, leaving him at a loss because of my reaction.

I have had many challenges before in this kind of work and always found a way, through patience and respect, to stay on top during a bad deal until it ended as a win-win. I can remember walking into the bathroom next to the event room and letting the water run into the sink as I lost sight of myself in the mirror. I watched my lips say,

"Fuck it . . . It's in the past . . . It's time to move on."

As far as I could tell, this person had no plan on how he was going to pay me back. This was not the way I had imagined eliminating myself from this kind of problem. It was time for me to put an end to these kinds of situations. It no longer felt safe or decent to be acting this way while trying to raise two little girls. I tightly held on to my self-discipline and walked out of the bathroom. If nothing else, I learned that day never to let anyone slow me down. Regardless of whether they've lied or stolen, it was up to me to choose how I would react. I chose to take a hit right on the chin. Then I counted my lucky stars for the clean stretch of time I had with a positive cash flow in the art of lending dirty dollars.

After the cage was all set up, I headed over to my office to sit and talk with Combat Zone's better half, my cousin Melissa George. Melissa and I had worked hand-in-hand aggressively during the last three weeks leading up to the event, tying up loose ends before the show. I wasn't going to attend Combat Zone 41. My immune system was low, and my family, along with Danielle and the doctors, thought it would be best if I stayed clear of high volumes of people. This was the first promotion I was going to miss in five years. But I knew Combat Zone was under control, which allowed me to stay clear of the event with comfort.

Later that evening, I had Danielle wrapped tightly in my arms on our couch, watching *Shawshank Redemption*, while our two little girls were upstairs fast asleep in their beds. I had truly hit my expiration date with Combat Zone MMA. I told Danielle that night that I was going to skip putting on a third show in July and that I would end the year with one more show at the end of September before I cashed out my fight chips. I ended that night reading a text from Melissa: "It was a great night of fights, smooth show packed with fight fans!"

The last day of April ended on a Monday with a forecast of an avalanche advisory. I took off for a hiking trip up north to spend the day on and off a beaten path with Shane and Derek Wakeen. We all walked on a hard, flat, beaten-down trail for about fifteen minutes until we drifted through the forest toward the sound of running water. The three of us decided to follow the water upstream; it was going to be a river hike up a mountain today. We continued climbing over snow and ice-covered rocks, boulders, and trees that had either fallen into or across the high fast-flowing river. It was early spring in the White Mountains with temperatures hitting the thirties as the wind blew lightly.

I spent most of that day sweating out as much chemo as I could. I was on a mission to gain as much strength as humanly possible before I had to head back to Mass General for my last cycle of chemo. I was once told "It's not how you start, but how you finish!" I had a plan for the month of June, and this hike was part of my training. We all sat underneath a gorgeous sky, looking out at a wild long-distance range of New Hampshire mountaintops that went on for miles and miles, overlooking the Wildcat Ski Resort. In the opposite direction was a close-up view of Tuckerman Ravine Chute covered with a thin coating of snow and ice. We dropped our backpacks and spread out on the side of a cliff to do nothing other than have lunch, a laugh, and an honest talk about life.

After lunch Derek started banging on a small djembe, causing a beat to echo off of the large mountain ledge that we were all sitting on. Shane began banging out a rhythm on a bongo that flowed into his brother's beat. I shook my way into the rhythm that Derek and Shane were losing themselves in. I held my right arm high with a black egg shaker in my hand, looking out at a jaw-dropping view. The three of us passed around each instrument, chanted like tribesmen, and made music at a high spot up in the White Mountains.

Then, on our way back down the mountain, I slipped and fell. I was crossing over a section of the river, and my body ended up a little more than halfway submerged under running water. The icy cold water had been carving through snow and ice for the past few months, and it cooled my body temperature down quickly. It was a great way to finish up the hike because it was hilarious. Shane was standing up on a rock looking down at me, bent over laughing hysterically with his GoPro still mounted on his head. Derek was standing behind me, laughing his ass off. The only concern I had was asking Shane, "Did you GoPro that?" He nodded yes, as we all laughed again!

Over the next three days, I worked on my property, fixing up our home. But it was time to step up my training and push myself to greater heights if I wanted to achieve the goal I had set for the month of June. I ended my week on Friday, May 4, training with Calvin down in Lawrence, Massachusetts, at IntenZe MMA / 978 Boxing Club. Calvin and I spent most of the morning working the heavy bags and working out on a pull-up bar. After a solid morning warm-up, Calvin asked me if I wanted to spar. I told Calvin we could go light. I didn't want to get all banged up before I had to head back into the hospital for the last cycle of treatment.

He and I stepped into a sixteen-foot homemade chain link cage and went at it for about forty-five minutes. My body started to feel like its old self again. I was not wearing two yellow Livestrong bands on each wrist for cancer awareness; I was actually living stronger and truer than I had ever done before in my life. I was doing it! I was waking up each morning, giving my own life 100 percent in every direction to a point where I no longer felt weakness inside of me.

Hospitals, doctors, nurses, medicine, treatment, family, friends, ideas, and life all meshed together into one big project. It was time to send the results of this experiment through the roof!

Project mode was now in full effect.

I finally snapped deep down inside. I had turned myself into a madman ripping into life while keeping my eye on one prize and one prize only: a lifestyle that I had been told didn't exist by numerous people throughout my short twenty-eight years. I had turned myself into what I would like to call a champion. There wasn't a single person on the face of this planet that could distract me from where I was headed.

I stepped out of my own way—the path was clear! The prize was waiting for me to get there. The game show *Survivor* had a million-dollar prize if you made it to the end, so I thought it would be nice to create my own prize for the end of 2012.

I woke up on May 5 ready to hunt! I needed to remind myself, by living it, that humans were at the top of the food chain. So I got dressed in some leafy camo wear from head to toe and capped my head with my dirty old black cowboy hat. I packed up a bag, grabbed my shotgun, and tossed some ammo into one of my cargo pockets, and out the door I went.

I met up with a good friend of mine, Ethan Conley, who I met through the MMA industry a few years back. He and I were going to head into the woods for a turkey hunt. We crept quietly through the woods as we made our way to the edge of the tree line, stopping about fifty yards short of an open field. We spotted two large male birds moving slowly across the field.

We set up a female decoy, and then Ethan set himself up, sitting upright and tight against an old dead tree stump. I was lying down on my stomach, all stretched out with the stock of a twelve-gauge shotgun tucked into my right shoulder, with the barrel resting on the top on my left hand. I was lying down about three feet away from Ethan's right side. Ethan began imitating turkey sounds with a mouth reed. After a few minutes, there was a female bird ten to fifteen yards in front of us clucking softly as she walked back and forth looking in our direction. Within minutes, the hen took off into the thicker part of the woods, and the two large male birds started to make their way toward the corner of the field. Both birds ended up only a few feet away from an opening that would allow for a clean shot.

I was still holding a stretched-out position, lying flat on my stomach, when Ethan whispered out of the corner of his mouth, "Are you gonna take the shot?" I stayed still and said nothing, waiting for the bird. I had my eye on one of the birds and was waiting for him to move clear of some low brush.

I squeezed the trigger and *BANG!* The bird flipped over backward, and Ethan yelled out, "Shoot the other one!" As I tossed the gun into midair toward Ethan, I yelled back, "You shoot 'im!" Ethan caught the weapon in midflight as he jumped onto his feet and tucked the stock into his shoulder . . . *BANG!* Bird number two was down.

We both sat with ear-to-ear smiles after a congratulatory handshake on our hunt. We watched the two toms flap their wings and roll around in the field as they slowly died before we retrieved our kill. It was a one gun, double bird kill. The actual hunt itself always outweighs the rewarding feeling of a clean kill.

The entire next day, Sunday, May 6, was focused on nothing more than my family, with my cell phone once again turned off before I headed back into Boston for my last and final cycle of treatment.

Chapter Five

Mindset of a Champion

On Monday morning, May 7, Danielle and I made another drive into Boston so I could check back in to Mass General for my fourth and final cycle of chemotherapy. I was ready to blast out the next five days of my life while still holding on tightly to the mindset of a champion.

I was told I had a new room this week on the cancer floor. I was also told that it had a great view of a city sunrise. The first thing I did once I stepped foot into my new room was start to rearrange my office to my liking. I hung Ava D.'s wind chime on my IV pole, taped up the pictures of my girls at the end of my bed, and then pulled out a large stack of cards all wrapped up with rubber bands. I collected all the cards that I had received from family and friends during the past ten weeks. It was my way of thanking each and every person for their support. It was also inspiring to look at all the cards lined up, knowing how important every person was to me who had signed a card. The lineup of cards was like a section of fans cheering me on in life, not cancer sympathy!

I worked out each day on the eleventh floor, which became my workout room during my time at Mass General. I was not going to let my treatment take over my inner strength. **I was going to stay hungry and strong** as I conditioned my body and mind, knowing that it was the only way I would be able to accomplish a goal I had set for early June. One of the most rewarding feelings I have found in my own life is accomplishing certain things without talking about the details to others.

All the time that I was going to be alone in my city office this week would be devoted to labeling footage and still shots as I structured out my future play by play. I also took the time to wander all over Mass General, burning off as much time as I possibly could while making week four seem like a complete blur.

I spent time in the hospital gift shop, trying on all different women's hats and reading glasses, making Danielle laugh over and over again. The greatest healing of all—your loved ones' sincere laughter. I spent a lot of time sitting and walking around the healing garden, which was in full bloom. There was a section of Mass General called the Bulfinch Building, and it was like a museum. I spent time in this particular part of the hospital and learned the history of Mass General, going back to the 1800s. I went for a walk to the café if I needed anything at all to eat or drink, mainly because of the distance it was from my room and the time it took me to get there. I felt time was getting used wisely this week. I spent more time quietly walking back and forth in the hallway with the Wall of Hope. I sucked on grape Popsicles and devoured lemon Italian ices all week and played with my children when they visited. I passed time sitting by my big picture window in my office chair, jamming on the harmonica as the sun shined brightly upon my face. I even had a music therapist stop by and teach me a few chords on a ukulele that she let me borrow. I had never played a stringed instrument before, and it was nice to sit and drift away to the soft sounds that the ukulele delivered every time I dragged my fingers over the strings.

There was kindness all around me when I was a patient at Mass General.

I found it inspiring that almost every nurse who worked on the Lunder Building's ninth-floor cancer unit came into my room at least once. I found great joy in meeting so many different people as time passed while I was a patient. I thought maybe it was Mass General's strategy to inspire patients—let them see, hear, and feel the touch of all the different helping hands. Whatever the reasoning was, I found it to be a wonderful experience.

My last morning at Mass General, I woke up nice and early hooked up to my trip drip. I witnessed the powerful sunrise the nurses and doctors had told me about. Friday's dawn sent piercing yellows and oranges in my direction like an explosion of brightness throughout the clustered city buildings.

My friend, best man, and first cousin, Captain Christopher Mark George, showed up for a surprise visit at Mass General, traveling all the way from across the country. He flew in to Boston from Fort Lewis, Washington State. Chris and I were talking on the phone, and I asked him when he thought he would be able to make it home for a visit. Then, what felt like half a second later, he walked right into my hospital room, laughing and giving me a firm handshake and big hug.

I was counting down the minutes while my last drip finished up. My room was filled with family members, and my office door was suddenly pushed open. A group of the Lunder Building ninth-floor staff came marching in with ear-to-ear smiles as the leader of the group held up a cake that had "Congratulations" spelled out in blue frosting. Along with the cake was a card signed by multiple people from the cancer unit.

It was uplifting to have so many positive people aiming their joy toward me. On Friday, May 11, I checked out of Mass General for the last time, with my LAST round of chemo COMPLETE!

The next morning I woke up at home feeling clear minded and ready to take on each second moving forward. I got up, showered, and ate a good, healthy breakfast with my family. I called up my younger sister, Mandy, to see if she wanted to go for an easy hike on some local trails to start off the morning. Mandy was nine months pregnant with her first child on the way, so I knew it would inspire me if she was up to go outdoors before she went into labor.

The sun was bright, and the air was fresh as Danielle, Ava D., and Kiana watched Auntie Mandy take long strides through plush-green fields. Watching my younger sister push herself mentally and physically started to inspire me in a huge way about the goal I had set for the Relay For Life next month. I found out about Relay For Life after my third cycle of treatment. I had never heard of the event before, and one of my and Danielle's good family friends, Lindsey Guselli, brought it to our attention. Her mother and father had a huge helping hand in organizing the event in the town I grew up in.

The relay started back in May 1985, when I was only two years old! I was told a doctor named Gordy Klatt walked and ran for twenty-four hours around a track in Tacoma, Washington. Since that day, Relay For Life has spread worldwide with millions of people participating and getting involved in this society, which has raised billions of dollars to help fight cancer.

I had three weeks to step up my training and sweat out as much chemo as I could before June 2 got crossed off my calendar. I was eating healthy, hiking, biking, kayaking, golfing, exercising, spending time with Danielle, and playing with our children as I continued to use the world as my gym. I was doing everything in life that made me feel good about who I was and what I believed in. I felt strong and secure in my mind and my body. I was told that the Relay For Life was going to start at one in the afternoon and go until seven the next morning. This was eighteen hours of walking around Methuen High School's track, remembering, celebrating, and fighting back against cancer.

Danielle had gone ahead and formed a team with eight of her childhood friends; they called themselves Eights For Life. Danielle believed in me, and now she had a team of people who also believed in me. There was, however, one person in my life who did not believe in me. He even brought it to my attention.

When my father-in-law heard I was going to walk for eighteen hours straight, he looked me straight in the eye when I was at his home and asked me about the walk. After I explained the Relay For Life and my intentions for the walk, he said, "You cannot walk for that long . . . you have to train for something like that. Plus, with everything you're going through . . . " He assumed all this instead of asking if I had been training. I paused in confusion. Then he turned and walked away as he said with a negative mannerism, "That's too much walking anyways."

It's amazing how much drive we can actually gain when somebody tosses doubt in the air. I've learned the best way to handle this kind of negativity in my own life is to silently thank that person for not believing in me and carry on with my head held high.

On June 2, New England woke up to more rain falling from the sky than I had seen all year. This was the morning of the Relay For Life. Rain or shine, we were walking! Everyone was wearing raincoats and rain boots, and hundreds of people were helping set up tents and tarps to stay dry throughout the event. It was one of the most positive experiences I have ever had. Some of us might have heard the phrase "walk it off," and we did exactly that.

Danielle had raised a little over seven thousand dollars for the relay. I ended up walking the full eighteen hours, which was about fifty-four miles straight. The rain was unforgiving; it fell throughout the night up until the last hour of the relay. The sky decided to open up after a slow and gloomy sunrise to the most spectacular shade of blue. Every storm eventually runs out of rain—this was incredibly symbolic for me, being a cancer survivor at an event that was designed to create cancer awareness.

The next morning, June 4, after walking fifty-four miles to celebrate life and death, I found myself back in a hospital. This time, I was looking down at my younger sister holding on to new life. I had become an uncle for the first time to a new little baby girl named Aliya Grace. I was a proud man that day as I stared hard into my niece's slow-opening infant eyes, letting myself fall in love with another precious little miracle wrapped up in pink!

The next three days I stayed in the comfort of my home, playing with my children while taking breaks to label and organize GoPro footage and make notes that would trigger certain memories when it came time to reflect back on my past.

On Friday, June 8, I suited up to attend a family wedding. After I snugged up my tie, I stared deep into the mirror at a bald man without any eyebrows. This man had no eyelashes or nose hairs and was pale white with an edematous face. I had no clue who I was looking at in the mirror. It was horrifying, yet comforting. Here I was in a hotel room, in my own space, staring at this person I had seen a million times before, yet I couldn't recognize him. I knew exactly what he was made of deep down inside, and after I went through the motions of watching this stranger get ready, I placed one foot in front of the other and made my way into a room filled with family and friends; many of them I had not seen since before I started chemotherapy.

I've had a lot of different looks over the years, whether it was long hair, short hair, facial hair, hats, glasses, or the kind of clothes I wore, which created a new reflection in the mirror each day.

The night of the wedding, I found it amusing how many people looked in my direction as if they had seen a ghost. I would make eye contact with certain individuals and then sense an unsure look in their eyes that made me smile. Some would even approach me with a lot of discomfort in their mannerisms. Almost as if I were contagious! They would say hello, ask how I was doing, and then walk away quickly before I could even ask how they were doing. Others approached me with comfort like they knew the man I was made of deep down inside. The day was filled with interesting moments that I will cherish forever.

The next week I started off my Monday morning back in a hospital. This time it was for CT scans, x-rays, and blood to be drawn. This was all being done for the first time since all that toxic chemo had absorbed into my body.

Three days later I was back at Mass General, sitting in front of Dr. Richard Lee. When the door opened, I could see that Dr. Lee had news to tell me about my scans that was going to cause tears to roll down Danielle's cheeks. After the doctor took a seat in front of us, I asked him how his children were doing. He said fine and then returned the same question. I continued to maze around the reason I was sitting in front of Dr. Lee. I finally blurted out, "So, how do the results look?"

Out of the corner of my eye, I witnessed tears dripping from Danielle's face after Dr. Lee responded with the word *surgery*.

On June 16, I was inspired by two beautiful people at my sister Jenni and Shane's engagement party. David and Diane Sollars were two of the few people that I had decided to share some of my ideas with after David had asked me, "What have you been up to?" I explained how I was in the process of creating a video journal to tell and show a detailed story with both written and video content tied together. David smiled and then responded, "Sounds brilliant!"

Diane was standing beside the two of us as David turned away to speak with someone else at the party. Diane and I started to have a conversation, and she said something to me that I will carry with me to the end of my time: "David, share your story with others, let it inspire, and let it take care of you and your family for the rest of your life." David and Diane are what I like to call a rare couple. When I think of the two of them, words like *genuine*, *intelligence*, *respect*, and *charisma* come to mind.

Despite having a really great time at the engagement party, it was a confusing weekend for me because of the news about my scans. I started off the third week of June back in a hospital, consulting with Dr. C, who had performed my first surgery. The one sentence that I do remember hearing was that a knife would be involved to remove the spotted shadows near my spine that were seen on the scans.

A decision had to be made regarding the surgeon, hospital, and procedure of this next surgery, which I called "the fish gutting." I was to be cut from the bottom of my sternum, straight down the middle of my stomach, and around my belly button, in order to remove the shadows around my lower spine. The plan of attack was to open me up wide enough to take out all of my insides in the midsection, in order to remove the affected lymph nodes near my spine as well as a few lymph nodes in the surrounding area to be safe. Then piece me back together.

The big question I had to answer was what surgeon to choose. One thing that raised a red flag for Danielle during our meeting with Dr. C was that he had only performed four of these surgeries.

After our appointment, Danielle immediately began researching this specific surgery, known as a RPLND, or retroperitoneal lymph node dissection. She found several urologists who had a great deal of experience with this surgery, specifically one who happened to be located in the Boston area. His name was Dr. Jerome P. Richie, and Danielle and I met with him on June 21, at the Dana-Farber Cancer Institute.

Dr. Richie was chief of urologic surgery at Dana-Farber/Brigham and Women's Hospital and was the Elliott C. Cutler professor of surgery at Harvard Medical School. The deal sealer was that he had performed hundreds of these surgeries.

I was ready to give Dr. C his fifth RPLND surgery, seeing that he had cut me the first time, and I liked him as a person, so it felt right. Plus, I figured Dr. Richie had had a fifth body count once too. But after the response I got from Danielle and a few other loved ones in my family, when they asked what my decision was going to be, I decided to call back Boston's highly respected and well-seasoned surgeon, Dr. Richie.

On Tuesday, June 26, I spent my day shopping for antiques. I was in search of some old furniture to finish up my remodeled front porch. I figured since the nice summer weather was moving into New England, I would be doing a lot of front-porch sitting after my fish gutting. This meant more thinking time before the stroke of midnight ending 2012!

The slow kill continues.

On Wednesday, June 27, I woke up with a let's-make-a-deal attitude. It was time to start selling off pieces of equipment that I now owned but still had the "Roy's" lettering on the doors. The best part of this process was that I was going to keep all the bullshit local. I called up a friend of mine that was a local lumberjack, who only lived a few blocks away from Ricky Roy, and asked if he would like to purchase the bucket truck off of me. The name of the local candidate was Dan the Tree Man. I mentioned to Dan, "Make me an offer and it's yours." All I was after was having my uncle's pride and joy rolling around the asphalt in his own neighborhood with a new name on the side of the truck to crush his twenty-five-year, ongoing ego trip.

The first piece of Roy's Tree Service's equipment . . . SOLD! The truck went for short change that no buyer would refuse. I chose to keep it real with a local lumberjack that I actually enjoyed being around. There was a reasoning behind my madness on why I chose Dan the Tree Man.

Danielle and I ended off the month of June with an open house for friends and family, with a cookout followed by a bonfire. One of our guests who showed up that night was artist Markus Sebastiano. His work has appeared in Boston's Museum of Fine Arts and many other wonderful places. Markus has been an inspiring artist and, more than that, a good friend of mine since our teenage years. When he pulled into our driveway, my older sister, Jenni, yelled to me, "David, come up here! Markus has something he would like to give you."

Markus handed me a large framed piece of mahogany that was three feet tall by two feet wide. There were famous quotes engraved on the front of the art piece. They were strategically placed by Markus, sending a message that allowed me to move ahead one space in the process of my own project.

> *Courage is not the absence of fear, but rather the judgment that something else is more important than fear. Feed your faith, and your fears will starve to death.*
>
> *The most beautiful people we have known are those who have known defeat, known suffering, known struggle, and have found their way out of the depths. These persons have an appreciation, a sensitivity, and an understanding of life that fills them with compassion, and a deep-loving concern. Beautiful people do not just happen.*
>
> *The tests of life are not meant to break you, but to make you.*
>
> *Out of difficulties grow miracles.*
>
> *When you're going through hell, keep going. The only way out is the way through.*
>
> *You're an inspiration to all those who know you. Your spirit is stronger than anything that can happen to it.*
>
> *As you shall think, so shall you become.*
>
> *You were born to win this fight.*

Monday morning I was up bright and early with the gas pedal to the metal in the fast lane. I was on my way into the city to fill out my paperwork at the Brigham and Women's Hospital in Boston before my upcoming surgery.

The Fourth of July was upon us before we knew it. This special day was the celebration of the birth of the United States of America as an independent nation. It was also the celebration of the birth of a special woman who has taught me everything I know about inner strength and kindness—my mother, Diane Marie Roy George!

After a night filled with exploding colors throughout a dark, clear sky, Danielle and I packed up the girls to head home. As my family and I were driving down the road, I realized my godparents, my aunt Mary and uncle Mark George, were flickering their headlights at us. Danielle and I pulled over as my uncle drove up and quickly leaned out of his window, passing a white envelope into our vehicle, saying, "David, we were holding on to this for you, but we want you to have it now." My uncle and aunt hollered, "We love you all," as they rode away in the opposite direction. The envelope my uncle handed me was thick and heavy. I waited until we were home and I had a quiet moment to myself to open the gift.

I opened the card to find a smooth charcoal-black stone. My aunt Mary had written out in the card "David, your uncle Mark picked up this stone from the beach to hold on to for inspiration when you were going through treatment. We want you to hold on to this black stone for your own inspiration and return it back to the beach when you feel the time is right!"

Immediately, that black stone became indispensable to my well-being in a superstitious kind of way. And I became extremely curious about why the stone was inspiring to my godfather. Uncle Mark was the person that put the word *work* into perspective for me at a young age, but he was also the person in my life to whom I owed a lifetime of gratitude for teaching me about confidence and how to laugh at almost everything life delivers.

I spent the rest of the night wide awake, thinking about why I was going to let a doctor slide a knife into the front of my body, right below the middle of my sternum, and then continue the incision down through the center of my abdomen, around my belly button, and further down past my pant line.

The most important thing that had to happen, though, was to be strong and focused for my three-year-old little girl, Ava D., my seven-month-old baby girl, Kiana, and the woman that I chose to share a life with, Danielle. All three of my girls were sound asleep in our old farmhouse on July 4. I stayed awake with a racing mind, as I listened to random fireworks blasting off late into the morning of July 5. Surgery day was here.

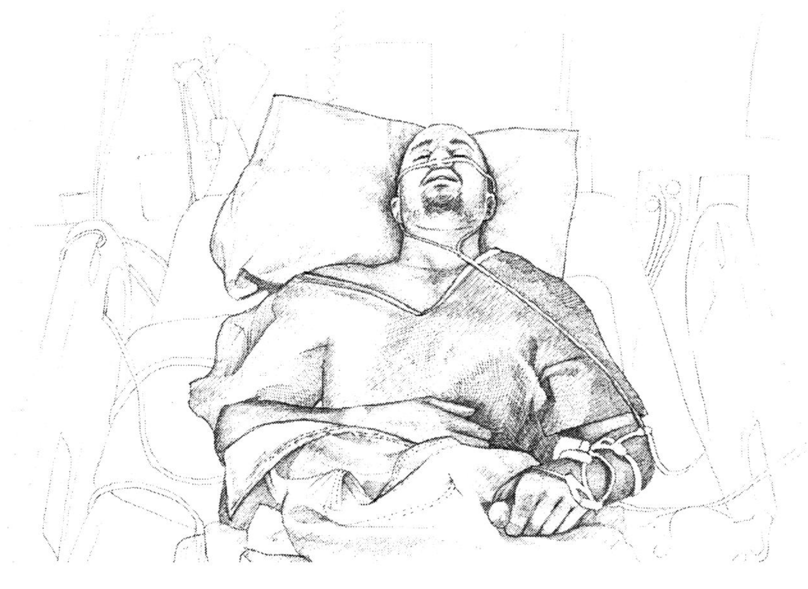

Chapter Six

Turtle Wins the Race

It was wild knowing that today was the last time I would ever look down at my stomach and see a smooth, seamless abdomen.

The last thing I can really remember was going into the bathroom fully dressed. I had a talk with the reflection in the mirror—two talks, actually—and then I changed into a johnny from the hospital. I took off all my jewelry, capped my head with a hat, and followed up with a quick clap, two step, double-elbow raise, sticking both thumbs up to the world! I was now ready for the next obstacle in my path, which went by the name of anesthesia.

Right before I was rolled away by the hospital staff to an operating room, I asked Danielle to please do me a huge favor. "Danielle, no matter what, will you make sure the GoPro is recording when you walk into the recovery room for the first time? No matter what," I repeated. She gave me her word. Then tears started to roll down her face as she took my hat off the top of my head, kissed me on my temple, and said, "I love you, David." Then I was rolled away down a cold, stale hallway.

Once the surgery was over and the mental fog started to clear out, the only thing I can remember happening was trying to open my mouth after slowly opening my eyes and trying to focus in on where I was. I had the worst cotton mouth ever; the middle of my bottom lip even split open after letting out a small yawn. I could not get over how dried out my tongue and lips were. Then Danielle walked over to my bedside as I continued to make a face like I was sucking on a lemon while moving my tongue all around my teeth and gums, trying to find some saliva. Danielle asked me how I was feeling, and I said in a dry voice, "I can barely talk. My mouth is so dry; can you find me some water?"

Danielle came back with a nurse who handed me a cup with a few straws in it. The cup was partially filled with water, and what I thought were straws were actually small sticks with a square-shaped sponge at the end. Danielle pulled one out of the cup and handed it to me. It looked like a piece of rock candy but was made to suck on and rehydrate the mouth.

I started brushing my teeth with them and scrubbing my tongue. Soon I could speak a little clearer, and I asked Danielle why she didn't have the GoPro running when my eyes first saw her. She started laughing and said, "David, are you for real right now?" I looked up at her and kind of clinched my eyebrows, confused.

She said, "I have already been in here twice with the GoPro and filmed you like you asked me to." I held that look of confusion as Danielle continued. "Wow! That's pretty crazy. You don't even remember seeing me, your mother, or your father?" I let out a small breath with a light laugh and said, "No, I don't, not at all. But you filmed me?" She replied, "Yes, I did, David." I nodded. **"OK, well, that is going to be an interesting clip to review later."**

The next few hours lying in my hospital bed consisted of swabbing my mouth with my sponge pops and pushing down on the small round button near my bed that forced morphine into my body. There was some real pain in my midsection after getting sliced open, but I enjoyed the high when the drug began to flow through my bloodstream.

Danielle asked me to stop pushing the button so often. "David, only push it if you need it." I'm well aware that there are few things in life we really need, but I sure as hell wanted what was in that bag beside my bed. I knew it would only be a matter of time before I would be unhooked from what the pharmacist had mixed up for me, so I was fueling on up!

Around ten that evening, my nurse came into my room. The first thing I asked her was "When can this plastic tube come out of the head of my penis? It really doesn't feel all that good." She said, "I bet it doesn't," and then explained that it had to stay in till at least tomorrow afternoon. I said nothing.

The nurse then said she wanted to see if I could get up and go for a walk. The thought of that was overwhelming. I had not eaten anything in the last twenty-four hours and was fogged out with anesthesia. I had been sliced open with a knife to the midsection, had my guts pulled out and then pushed back in, had my abdomen sewn back up, and had my veins pumped up with morphine while I sucked on wet sponge pops for the last ten hours. I was absolutely wiped out mentally and physically.

I asked Danielle to set up the GoPro and get this on film. I wasn't sure how it was going to actually go, so I wanted to make sure it was documented. It was wild how slow my body moved in the upright position. It felt like my stitched-up stomach was going to burst open as I tried to use my core to get myself sitting up with my feet off the edge of the bed and onto the floor, ready to go for my first stand.

Danielle and my nurse helped me to my feet and closed up the back side of my johnny. I ended up taking a few slow steps and made it out into the hallway, with once again another IV pole shadowing me along the way at the pace of a tortoise.

I crept my way down a hectic, fast-paced hospital hallway. "The turtle wins the race," I said before I began taking baby steps in my hospital slippers while wearing tight white TED anti-embolism stockings, which stopped right below my kneecaps, and still my johnny, of course. My hair was slowly growing back from the chemotherapy treatments as a whitish-gray color on my head and face. I had also removed my contact lenses and was wearing my glasses. I felt like an absolute geezer, but I was only in my late twenties. I made eye contact with other patients and hospital staff members while moving on by with my IV pole following closely, as I randomly nodded and smiled at others while taking life one step at a time.

After three days of moving at the pace of a tortoise while recovering at the Brigham and Women's Hospital in Boston, I was finally discharged.

I was back in the comfort of my home, lying in my bed with my cell phone next to my ear on the pillow. I had been invited to listen in on a leadership conference call hosted by one of the most inspiring serial entrepreneurs that I personally know, David Sollars! He is also one of my greatest mentors. I was fired up to be involved in this conversation. It was an empowering first day home as I listened to the wisdom travel out of the speakerphone and into my own thoughts as I lay in my bed, drifting into my own world of possibilities.

Mr. Sollars had explained on his invite that the leadership conversation was going to be geared to the process of becoming a published author. It was quite interesting to me, given the details I had shared with David about my own project a few weeks ago. Mr. Sollars is a published author, and he also had a guest speaker on the line, Bill Gottlieb, who was labeled as a best-selling health author.

Bill explained that he had over thirty years of experience in the industry and had written thirteen books, selling over two million copies worldwide in five different languages. After hearing this, I figured it would be a wise idea to listen up. Halfway through Bill's presentation, Mr. Gottlieb gave an example that enhanced the vision I had for my own project.

Bill's tone of voice started to change. You could practically feel the passion and see the mannerism of his voice slowly start to trickle out of the speakerphone as he described what gave him, a best-selling author, his drive. In his own words, he explained that when he was working on one of his books, he had envisioned himself sitting there writing in the middle of a large stadium with two million people cheering him on!

My blood pressure rose after hearing Bill explain himself that way. I remember clinching my fist and nodding my head while saying out loud, with pure adrenaline, **"THAT'S WHAT I'M TALKING ABOUT."** I've had many of my own moments, looking hard and deep into the lens of the GoPro, during my own process of filming, gathering content, and securing ideas. I have envisioned millions among millions of people fist pumping and hollering with joy, like a bunch of screaming, hungry fans with an appetite for more of what I was creating. I had never met Bill Gottlieb before, but he now had a huge, uplifting part in the rest of my journey in the world of writing.

On July 11, my father showed up at my home. He handed me a small package the size of a postcard. Inside was a letter and a gift from a woman I didn't know. My father told me that somebody he knew asked him to please pass this package off in my direction. I tore the top of the package open and dumped out a string of rosary beads.

I've always enjoyed the style of rosary beads and really liked the look of these particular ones. I unfolded a white piece of paper that went along with the gift. The note explained that a woman named Donna Corso made a trip to the Holy Land, where she had met a priest from Poland during her travels. He was celebrating his fifth anniversary as a priest and had received special permission to perform mass inside the Tomb of the Holy Sepulchre (not the big church by that name, but the actual small tomb in which some believe Jesus was laid and rose from the dead). The priest invited Donna to attend the mass. She was one of a few people, as the space was so small. The note read that the rosary beads I was given were laid down in the tomb and blessed.

I have already explained my beliefs in religion, and I know for sure that I held my head high and proud after putting those beads around my neck. The power and strength of this kind of gift came from the fact that somebody I didn't even know was acting out of the kindness of her heart for my well-being, halfway across the world in an ancient tomb.

Two days later the warm summer sun was shining bright as we celebrated Ava D.'s third birthday as a family of four. I sat underneath a bridge and watched my family play in the sand and splash around in the brackish water. Every so often a loud alarm would sound off, causing all vehicles at each end of the bridge above us to stop. The bridge would slowly open upward, allowing large vessels to float on by. I think it's good to crawl under a bridge every once in a while. What I mean by this is that isolation can be an incredible thing when shared with your loved ones.

I had a lot on my mind the next few days after Ava D.'s birthday. I couldn't stop thinking about how fast three years had passed. On Monday, July 16, I woke up bright and early, showered, scrubbed my tusks, and stepped into a pair of light grayish swim trunks. I pulled on a gray tank top, draped my new rosary beads around my neck, slipped into a pair of sandals, and capped my head with an old cloth Kangol hat. I was headed to the beaches to take care of something extremely important. I had spotted this specific location that I wanted to go to when I was relaxing underneath the bridge while enjoying my family.

I kicked my sandals off when I reached the sand that touched the Atlantic Ocean. I continued on my way, walking and stepping and leaping from rock to rock, boulder after boulder, into a light mist of sea salt, heading for a location that ended with a view of open water.

As I approached the end of this path, there were three young men, probably ranging in age from eleven to fourteen, at the end of the rocks. One of them had on a black T-shirt with colored lettering on the front. I caught a quick glimpse of the top portion of his shirt. It read, in big bold white capital letters across his chest, "COOL!" Under the word *cool* was the word *story* in blue capital letters.

I quickly asked if he would mind holding the GoPro in my direction as I stood at the end of the rocks. This random human at the end of a jetty now had a hand in helping me tell my story.

I had headed to the beach that morning to take care of something important. I set out to think deep about two questions that David Sollars had slipped into my thoughts. He asked me, "What would make somebody want to read your story? What is it that makes you and your story different from other cancer-survivor stories?" Then he followed up by saying, "Let that marinate for a while," as he grinned.

I sat by the water's edge on the rocks and thought pretty damn deep about my upcoming appointment with Dr. Jerome Richie in two days. This was when he would tell me if I had to undergo any more chemotherapy or surgeries moving forward. My thoughts began to drift away into the unknown as the sun set through the tall sea grass.

Two days passed, and Danielle and I drove back into Boston. We sat beside one another in a hospital office, waiting for Dr. Richie to deliver the news.

Dr. Richie walked into the room and sat down in front of me and Danielle. He asked me to stand up and pull up my shirt. He started checking out my scar and pushed on my stomach and said, "Looks to be healing well." The doctor then got up and acted as if he was about to walk out of the room. Right before doing so, I asked him if he knew what my final results were. He turned back and said, "Oh yeah, I don't know. Let me go check and see if they are even in yet." A few minutes later Dr. Richie popped his head back into the room, quickly announcing, "Everything looks good. All results negative! No more chemo or surgeries." Dr. Richie shook my hand, smiled, and then complimented my hat.

Danielle began crying out of happiness. I nodded my head in front of the doctor, a stone-cold look on my face, and said, "OK." Danielle gave me a tight hug and kissed me on the face as I still stood there in shock from the news.

The speed of the news happened fast, from hearing three words come out of one doctor's mouth, "You have cancer," to a different doctor casually walking into a room saying three different words, "All results negative." I was so fucked up in the head walking out of Brigham and Women's Hospital that afternoon. I stopped at the entrance and asked Danielle if she could take a picture of me standing next to the hospital sign.

I had a feeling inside of me like **I had lost something**, which I did—my mind! I didn't say much on our drive home. We stopped at Danielle's parents' house to pick up the girls on our way.

During the last few days of July, I tipped my hat to my children. Kiana started crawling and Ava D. climbed her first mountain—eight hundred and seventy-four feet to the highest point next to the largest body of water in the state of New Hampshire. Progress was happening in every direction with a good vibe each morning as my granddaddy clock kept ticking away, minute after minute, toward the new year.

I started off August by putting myself back into lumberjack mode. It had been a long seventeen-week stretch of not answering any calls regarding tree work, and I'd left all my equipment that I still owned in the parked position. I felt it was best to embrace the last few months of owning a tree service before I struck a deal with a buyer to put Roy's Tree Service out of its misery. I truly enjoyed the lifestyle as a lumberjack: climbing trees, operating a log truck, hauling loads of fresh-cut lumber to the sawmill, running a chainsaw, bucking up logs, and splitting firewood. Even the smells and sounds of the trade were a huge part of who I was and what I was made up of over the past seventeen years.

I created a new model of how I was going to operate the tree company for the remaining months. I called a few well-seasoned woodpeckers that I knew locally and bumped up my payroll substantially to surround myself with high-caliber lumberjacks to complete each job I booked. I made sure of one thing though: there would be no long-term deals made with any woodpeckers as time moved on. I was now a fly-by-night tree guy in search of the correct buyer as I continued to diminish a twenty-five-year, up-and-running company to create a window of time to pursue a vision in my life that continued to grow stronger and grander each morning I rose.

On Monday, August 6, I had no fucking clue what I was doing. I showed up in Boston and walked back into Mass General. I had set up a meeting with Dr. Richard Lee. The sole purpose of the meeting was to explain to him how I had been filming myself during my time at the hospital. I didn't have anything else on my mind or reason for setting that meeting up except to leak out something that I was working on to Dr. Lee.

I spent the rest of the day walking around the city of Boston. I watched tour boats go by in the harbor and small sailboats slice through the dirty water in the light wind. I sat on a bench at a ball field that had "Curse Reversed 2004" engraved into the front of it in honor of the Boston Red Sox winning the world series. I lay on my back in the plush-green grass in the outfield, looking up at the sky, trying to wrap my head around the last few months.

Progress was still happening at a pretty good pace. On Wednesday, August 8, I completed my first set of ten pull-ups after my surgery. I spent most of my day hitting golf balls into the forest behind my home. The twisting motion was a fantastic stretching and strengthening exercise for my midsection as my insides continued to slowly heal. One of the most difficult tasks I was still having trouble with was bending down to slide on a pair of socks. I would have to say that I definitely enjoyed not being able to do this at times because Ava D. became aware that her pops had a hard time with this, and it was something she was excited to help me with each morning. Looking down at my three-year-old as she worked my stockings over my toes because I was in pain was priceless.

I spent the next ten days hiking on trails, climbing up small mountains, Rollerblading, biking, doing pull-ups and push-ups, swinging a golf club, and driving around as a salesman looking at tree jobs. Most of all, though, I put in hours of some good front-porch sitting, relaxing in a rocking chair, talking and laughing with my girls.

Saturday, August 18, was a day I will remember for a lifetime. I watched the three most adorable females in my life enjoy Mother Nature at her finest. The sun shined bright with overhanging trees casting shadows all around. There were holes and basins carved into the New Hampshire ledge with smooth, polished surfaces that had a mirrorlike image to the eye, as a low-running brook named Lucy flowed by continuously. The sparkling, crystal-clear water flowed over a series of rocks and ledges, creating small waterfalls scattered along what was once an operating sawmill back in the late 1800s. This marvelous wonder of a spot we decided to picnic at was called Diana's Baths.

I spent the following week lightly exercising and then more time in a rocking chair as I labeled and organized GoPro footage and still shots.

On Saturday, August 25, I spent the day fixing up a piece of property that my old man had bought a few months back. My older sister, Jennifer, asked if I could help her out by spending some time cleaning up the property so she and Shane could be wed there. The property had a log cabin, where my father was spending some of his time to get away from my mother! It became a place he could clear his head and spend his time with new company.

One week later I fell into an interesting mindset.

On September 2, I woke up a proud man and a sad man. I was wearing pink on this fine day. The same color pink many of our eyes see when we think about awareness for breast cancer. That was the color of my tie that I wore with a black tuxedo and a peacock feather pinned to my right collar. I had a silver pocket watch tucked away into my jacket pocket that was a gift from my future brother-in-law. I stood strong in front of a gathering of family and friends celebrating the marriage between Jenni and Shane, on a piece of property that in my eyes signified the opposite of words like *love*, *loyalty*, and don't forget *forever* in my parents' relationship. I felt a vibe of sadness each time I made eye contact with my mother that day. It's absolutely amazing how well a facial expression can tell a story about a loved one's emotions.

Whether I felt proud or sad, I felt honored to stand beside two important people, my big sister and brother-in-law, who I will always associate with words like *love*, *loyalty*, and once again, not to forget about *forever*.

Mr. and Mrs. Wakeen were the reason that the dance floor was packed, the music was loud, the champagne and wine bottles were popping, and the liquor was overflowing in glasses while a bonfire blazed until four in the morning. Everyone was celebrating and reminding each other to cherish the vibe of passionate love surrounded by good company.

The next day I was back in Combat Zone mode.

I hit the pavement hard on Monday morning as a town worker once again, pounding in street signs for my upcoming fight night. The next morning I got things organized for fighter weigh-ins and set up my cage for Combat Zone MMA 42 (CZ 42)!

All the fighters I had booked showed up on Thursday, September 6, and made weight, and most of them seemed focused and ready to compete. The next day was a big day for me as a fight night that was going down in history in my book. This was going to be my last "Friday Night Fights at the Rock," at least the last one I would ever put any effort into again. CZ 42 was the night that I became the champ of my own show, and nobody even knew it but me. After six years of promoting live cage fighting, I never went into the cage to take any kind of photograph. But this show was different. Danielle had been to most of our events up until we had children. I asked her to please find a babysitter for our girls so she could attend the fights. After each bout the winner, since day one, takes a photo beside the round-card ring girls. At the end of tonight's show, I asked Danielle to step into the cage with me so we could have our picture taken. Victory was all I knew on September 7 in the fight game.

The next week I found a buyer and made a deal, which allowed me to hang up my hat in the fight game. I had tossed the white towel up in the air in my world of organized fighting. There was only one fight left in me, and it was the main event in my own life. I was now marketing and promoting this bloodbath of a fight I called "Reality vs. Dreams," and it was a fixed bout for a win-win!

I woke up bright and early on September 8 and headed to the coast. This was also the morning the Atlantic Ocean swallowed up the past twenty-six days of my life. I spent the day surfing with two childhood friends, and **my GoPro Hero was torn off my surfboard by my arm and sunk to the ocean's bottom**. After I got out of the water, I realized when I looked in my camera bag that I had left a full SIM card inside of my GoPro that now belonged to what covers 71 percent of the Earth—salt water.

Later that night when reviewing my Wildlife 2012 calendar, which I was using to mark off my progress with my project, I realized that I had never backed up any of the video content dated back to August 13. I then quickly opened up my hard drive labeled

"GoPro Project," and it was confirmed. I'd fucked up. Ironically, on August 13, I was out at sea, floating around to the motion of the ocean in a vessel with a fishing rod in my hand. Twenty-six days later, on September 8, I was out at sea on a surfboard. My lost content started at sea and ended in the sea.

So the next morning I drove straight to the store before I even took a shower and bought a brand new GoPro Hero. I even took photographs of the new GoPro still in its box. The mindset I had during this photo shoot was, What would GoPro be willing to do for me if I continued to build a project that marketed their product in such a unique way? If there is one thing I learned running the business of Combat Zone MMA, it is that you actually have to accomplish making a sponsor feel proud, visually and verbally, to hold a win-win relationship. In my eyes, GoPro was this project's title sponsor, and they didn't even know it yet.

The most important lesson I have learned in business is no one is entitled to a good deal. I'm well aware we can be turned down, laughed at, or ignored, but it all seemed worth a try to line up as many win-win deals as I possibly could during the making of *The Year It All Made Sense*. Even if the companies I was trying to target didn't know me from a hole in the wall, I thought if I strived to shine brighter than bright in the world of business and marketing, then I had a pretty damn good shot of sitting down in front of some new faces, with new inspiration, in the near future. I might even end up possibly shaking some of their hands, confirming a win-win, if I gave it my all.

I only had one hundred and fifteen days left to try as hard as I possibly could before my granddaddy clock smacked twelve, putting an end to the year.

I woke up in lumberjack mode the next morning. I put on a pair of black Dickies work pants, tucked in a white tank top, laced up a pair of steel-toe Chippewa boots, and spent the day bucking up logs and splitting firewood. The only thing on my mind today was my lost footage. I couldn't seem to stop replaying what kind of ideas, conversations, and visuals had sunk to the ocean's bottom. It was a strange feeling, trying to reflect back on the last twenty-six days. I even thought to myself, "Maybe it happened for a reason; maybe it was time to take the content that I did have and turn that into a finished project." It was a strange day bucking logs.

The next day I headed back to the coast with my family. I waxed up a surfboard and paddled out into the flat, calm water. There wasn't a wave in sight. I floated around in the spot where I had lost my GoPro as I watched my family play on the beach. I wasn't quite sure the exact reason for putting myself in the same location I was three days ago, but it felt right, so I did it.

When I paddled myself back to shore and sat down in the sand beside my family, I looked at Danielle and told her the thought that passed through my head when I was splitting firewood. I told her **maybe it happened for a reason**. She asked, "Maybe what happened for a reason?" I said, "Losing all that footage; maybe it's time to turn the material I do have into a finished project." Danielle looked at me and smiled like she knew something I didn't. I started laughing and said, "What?" She said, "David! Finish your project!"

I laid my head down that night, thinking back to what had been ingrained into my brain since childhood. "Do everything you say you're going to do in life." Danielle put the phrase in perspective for me when she told me to finish what I had started.

On September 12, my eyes opened early in the morning, and I headed out the door, ready to attack Mother Nature in a way that I had been avoiding since I fell from that small spruce tree back on December 1, 2011. I was going to put myself back up in a tree today. It had been nine months since I had climbed up a tree. My stomach felt strong, and more than anything I was craving to feel free and at peace like never before.

After about a month of a few scattered days hitting the ground as a salesman in the tree industry, I had decided to actually book one of the jobs I landed. The two lumberjacks that I called in for a day's pay showed up bright and early, ready to kill some trees. The log truck, dump truck and wood chipper, and crane all rolled out of the woodyard in single file, rolling past Robert Frost's old farmhouse, on this marvelous morning.

I became addicted immediately to being back up in a tree and feeling free and at peace. I booked two more jobs right away for the next two days so I could swing around in trees, with a chainsaw hanging from my hip as an undertaker to good old Mother Nature.

September 15 was a day I was looking forward to writing about before it even happened. I spent the whole day with Danielle from sunrise to sunset. We got up first thing that morning to head up north. I did my best to make sure a lot of blocks on my calendar were dedicated to spending time with the girl I fell in love with and chose to share a life with.

The weather was below average up north on Lake Winnipesaukee. We were both dressed for eighty-degree weather, but it was about fifty degrees on this morning. Danielle and I tossed on some life jackets, hopped onto a Jet Ski, and blasted all over the grandest body of water in the state of New Hampshire, chasing a huge white boat with the name "Mount Washington" on both sides of it. The cruise boat looked like something you would see in a Mark Twain book.

We glided through the freshwater, slowing down to a floating stillness, and then killed the engine and witnessed something neither one of us had ever seen before. The air was cold and the wind was ripping across this wide open section of the lake we were in. There were about sixty or more large sailboats slicing through the choppy, whitecapped water. I relaxed on the seat of the Jet Ski as I watched Danielle smiling as she floated around in the cold, rough water.

Eventually she and I docked up, dried off, changed, and headed to a place called Weir's Beach to grab some grub. We laid out a towel and had lunch. We tossed french fries in the air to flocks of seagulls as we dined beside a historical stone-built bridge by the water's edge.

I will say one thing from this experience. After having children, it's wild how important it is spending time with somebody who makes you feel good about yourself. After years and years of spending time with Danielle, she doesn't seem to get old. We folded up the blanket and stopped at the batting cages, and I chased her around a go-cart track in a green cart, screaming out her name, letting out "woo-hoos" lap after lap until I crossed the finish line!

The wind started to die down, and the sun began to break up any overhead clouds. We drove around the lake and stopped at a dirt parking area off the highway. Danielle pulled up her laces and tied her sneakers. She was waiting for me to do the same thing so we could hike to the top of a mountain. Halfway up the side of Mount Major, she picked up a rock and carved two letters into a birch tree growing out of a ledge on the mountain. It read "DG" with a heart and then the word "ME" with an exclamation point, all scratched into the white bark. We continued upward and onward until we reached the peak.

My day ended with a few candles burning on a small round ice cream cake and the singing of happy birthday to me after we tucked in our two little angels upstairs. Danielle treated me like a king on the night of September 15, 2012.

I spent the next day running a chainsaw, knocking down small maple trees to the left of our pond, and creating new scenery behind our home. I was tired of walking into my backyard and looking at the same view. This was the starting point to a project that was inspired partially by my two daughters. I knew my dump truck and wood chipper weren't going to be around for much longer since I was still searching for a buyer. So I figured it would make sense to pencil myself in on the jobs-to-do list.

I ended my day opening up my emails to take a look since it had been a few weeks without reading any of them. There was a message in my inbox from Caitlin Moore with the game show *Survivor*!

I began reading her email: "Hi David. *Survivor* premieres tomorrow and I couldn't help thinking about you. How are things with you? I hope you're well. Give me an update whenever you get a chance. Sending good thoughts your way! :) Cheers, Caitlin Moore, Casting Producer *Survivor* 25."

I wrote her back right away: "WOW! Thanks for checking in. I can't believe it has been about seven to eight months. I'm doing great! Like **sky's the limit** great! About eight weeks cancer-FREE! Here is a family photo on the top of Mass General, in their outdoor garden. That was into my third week of chemo. Living Strong! Believe it or not—you guys might like this since you're in the world of filming people—I have GoPro'd the majority of my journey through cancer. I have over 1,100 clips that range from three minutes to forty-five minutes over the last eight months. I guess I couldn't let go of the GAME! Survivor 2012! Thank you for remembering me. And hope to hear from you soon! Thanks, David A. George."

Survivor was starting to make some pretty good progress back into my life. Two days later Kiana was making some pretty good progress of her own. Our little baby girl went from crawling to getting up on her feet and taking eleven short steps. Danielle and I were both lucky enough to have witnessed this priceless, precious progress together.

The next day I sat in my crane picking treetops all day as I daydreamed about giving *Survivor* another shot. After I cleaned up and had dinner with my girls, I sat down in front of my computer and noticed another email from Caitlin Moore: "Hey, David! So glad you wrote back and gave me the update. I've been thinking of you, especially with all of this *Survivor* buzz going on, and I'm glad to hear you're doing well. So amazing you've been filming your journey. The best news is that you're currently cancer-free. So happy for you. Definitely keep me posted on your progress. When you feel healthy enough to give *Survivor* another shot, I'll be here and I've got your back. Take care of you and stay in touch! Cheers, Caitlin."

On September 22, New England officially made its crossover from summer into fall. Danielle and I raked leaves and stopped by a local farm and picked out pumpkins, gourds, hay bales, chrysanthemums, and cornstalks to decorate our home. We also built scarecrows with the help of Ava D. as Kiana supervised from her high chair. The best purchase from the farm was the two wooden signs that I grabbed from the cash-out section. One sign read, "Those who mind don't matter, and those who matter don't mind." The other read, "Never get so busy making a living that you forget to make a life." I had no idea who said either of these quotes, but they spoke loudly to me, and I wanted them to be in my home.

The next morning Danielle and I went on a small road trip to Maine. We cheered on my cousin Bill "the Bull" Murray in a bodybuilding competition. On our way home, we stopped at the outfitters Cabela's to purchase some new footwear for a hike Danielle and I were going to do next month for cancer awareness, in honor of Livestrong Day.

I spent the next two days as a heavy-equipment operator, running my twenty-eight-ton Manitex boom-truck crane, taking down some colossal-sized New England red oak trees on one of my own jobs. It's a wild mindset to be a crane operator on a tree removal job. The operator has the life of a climber on the end of the crane's cable all day long. Hand signals are the way of communication between both the operator and the climber, and when each person becomes comfortable working with the other, hand signals are rarely used, and the flow of work becomes effortless, due to a certain level of experience, safety, and skill. This allows the thrill of adrenaline on every single cut and pick in the business to be enjoyable.

The next morning I started phase two of the project behind my home. I worked on my property all day, ripping out all the stumps where the small maple trees once stood. Then the following day I put myself on the climbing end of the cable of a ninety-ton Grove crane with one thing on my mind—"safety first"—as the crane operator raised me one hundred and ninety-eight feet above solid ground. This shiny $1.5 million rig was brought in as a rental for the job so we could reach over a septic system and pluck out pine trees in the homeowners' backyard so a swimming pool could be installed. Days like today were the reason I felt addicted to helmets, chaps, eyewear, earplugs, spikes, harnesses, carabiners, ropes, chainsaws, and most of all heights.

I ended off September looking down at a fancy cake. It had a picture of a bottle of champagne with the cork blowing off. The words "Poppin' Bottles" were spelled out in frosting beside the picture. There was a yellow band wrapped around the base of the cake and carved into the band was the word "LIVESTRONG."

I thought hard about what this yellow world was becoming in my own life, ever since I put the Livestrong bands around my own wrists as I was going into my second cycle of chemotherapy. Lance Armstrong had become an interesting person to me for some reason or another as time passed. I created my own twisted-up inspiration in a positive way for both Lance and the Livestrong Foundation. I never forgot the mindset I gained once I slipped those two yellow bands on my wrist.

I thought back to one day a few years ago after putting on my Livestrong bands, while sitting in a Jiffy Lube, waiting to get an oil change, when I saw a magazine opened to an article that read, "Lance Armstrong is the most famous cancer survivor ever!" My eyes were always closed pretty tightly to the word *cancer*, but what I couldn't seem to wrap my head around at the time was, **How does one become the most famous cancer survivor ever?**

Dr. Richard Lee had dropped the Armstrong name at our first meeting before I had even received any chemotherapy. He said, "David, don't go out and buy or read the Lance Armstrong story *It's Not About the Bike* when you walk out of here." I laughed and said, "OK." I did ask Dr. Lee why, though, and he explained that it made chemotherapy sound awful. After that conversation, I thought back to when I was sitting in that Jiffy Lube, pondering about Armstrong being the most famous cancer survivor ever. I wondered if it was because he could ride a bike really fast or because he had a published book about his life story and explained his journey with cancer in a positive way to share with others. Either way, Lance Armstrong was a guy that I had never met before and didn't know from a hole in the wall, but he had an impact on my mindset about cancer, and he became an inspiration in my own life because of everything he has done for cancer awareness.

Now back at my house, as I looked down at this fancy cake with the champagne bottle and the yellow band around the base, I started to realize how many people in my own life, who I cared about, began wearing the bands around their own wrists. It was uplifting to slowly watch as time moved forward. I looked up and focused in on my wife, Danielle, standing beside my younger sister, Mandy, and my older sister, Jenni. The three of them were standing there smiling at me as I hovered over flickering candles. The three of them were the reason behind tonight's celebration.

Chapter Seven

Live True

The New England fall foliage had arrived, and October 2 marked the official Livestrong Day. Danielle and I packed up the truck with backpacks full of extra clothes, light snacks, and hiking shoes and headed north up Route 93 to Mount Washington. The car ride up to the White Mountains revealed a view bursting with the most vibrant, colorful foliage my eyes had seen in a long time.

Our plan was to hike all 6,288 feet. After three hours into our hike, we came upon a considerably older gentleman who looked to be maybe in his late seventies, slowly making his way up the mountain with the help of a walking stick. As I passed by him on a pretty gnarly ledge, it was quite clear he was pushing himself. Once our eyes met, I smiled and said, "How's it going?" The gentleman grinned and said, "Very good! But . . . when I hit pain and agony, only then will I go back down."

About half an hour later, Danielle and I spotted a couple that appeared to be taking a breather on the side of the rocky trail. Danielle said in a soft voice, "Hi, how's it going?" The woman had a concerned look on her face, explaining in a Canadian accent that she thought her husband had broken his ankle. We then noticed that his foot was stuck in a small crack in the trail as he lay there on his side in obvious discomfort.

She explained they'd been there for some time now and that they had not seen any other hikers and didn't have any cell service. "Do you have a phone?" the lady asked. I had left my cell phone behind, but luckily Danielle had her phone packed away in her bag. She unzipped her bag and pulled out her cell and handed it over to this couple in need of help. The woman immediately dialed 911, and we learned that this man was no stranger to ankle pain as he started to explain previous injuries he'd had to the same ankle.

Danielle and I decided to stay for a while and ended up having lunch since we were stopped anyways. We took advantage of the break to change into some warmer gear as the temperature was rapidly dropping. The 911 operator got the couple in touch immediately with park rangers in the area. They were told help could be there in about an hour or so. The woman asked if we would stay with them so they could have that security of the cell phone.

I looked at Danielle quickly and said quietly, "All they need is your phone that has service." They were dry, safe, and help was on the way. We had woken up that morning with a goal to touch the peak of this grand mountain. We had about another hour and forty-five minutes or so to go, plus the hike down. We'd run out of daylight if we stayed for sure. The couple told us they were staying at a nearby hotel at the base of the mountain. Danielle took down their information, and we told the couple we would meet them back at their hotel later on, but in the meantime they could keep the cell phone. Everyone seemed satisfied with this plan, so Danielle and I hiked on.

About forty-five minutes into hiking, we spotted a park ranger dressed in all green, running down the trail toward us. He was the fourth person we'd seen all day on the trail. Once he approached us, he asked, "Any chance you saw an injured man?" I responded, "Yup, about forty-five minutes right down the trail you're on. The guy said he hurt his ankle and can't stand on it. We left them our cell phone."

The ranger asked, "Are you planning on going to the top?" I said, "Yes, we are." He looked concerned and then said, "OK, well, there is some harsh weather moving in quickly, so you might not want to come back down the trail you came up." He told us to take a trail named Jewell. He informed us that it would bring us back down to the same location, but the weather would most likely be better on that side of the mountain. The ranger took off in a light jog down the trail.

Close to ten minutes after the ranger passed us, Danielle and I approached a yellow sign pounded into the ground that read,

"Some of the worst weather in America has been recorded here." The winds started to pick up speed, and the clouds began to circle above. Such an appropriate place for Mother Nature to start pushing back after we read that sign!

We ended up reaching the peak of Mount Washington. I left my Livestrong band, which had been on my wrist since the start of my chemo treatments, under the top rock of a pile of small stones stacked into the shape of a pyramid. We snapped a few photos at the highest point in the White Mountains and then began our hike down.

The park ranger was right about weather moving in. Heavy fog clouds started rushing up the side of the mountain, and the wind began to pick up, causing a constant mist to swirl around in the air. I couldn't even see Danielle ten to fifteen yards in front of me because the fog had gotten so thick at times. Close to an hour into our descent, the mist, wind, and fog let up, and the colors were so vibrant again all around us. The sun slowly started to drop as the trail flattened out and became easier on the body with only about one hour until we hit the parking lot. The sound of running water in the distance was getting louder and louder with each step forward. The sunlight had vanished quickly, making for a pitch-black finish.

I stopped in my tracks, and then Danielle stopped and said, "What's wrong?" I said, "Nothing—listen to that water flow." I stood silently and closed my eyes. Danielle said, "Come on, it's dark. Let's keep moving." The beaten-down dirt path guided us to a bridge that crossed the flowing river. I leaned over the side of the wooden bridge and looked into darkness. The railing on the bridge was damp to the touch as warm air surrounded us. The moon hadn't even shown its glow yet, as I looked up into the black sky. At this moment, it felt like we had hiked ourselves into the ending of a New Hampshire poem. Danielle said again, "Come on, David. It's getting late." It was back to the beaten path, with **the melody of a mountain river** slowly fading behind us, until we could hear only our own footsteps through the dark forest.

Once we got to the truck, we both changed into some comfortable, dry clothes and headed over to the hotel where the Canadian couple told us they were staying. Because the weather had forced us to use a different trail to come back down, we hadn't passed them and could only hope they'd gotten down safely. They were not at the hotel. We drove to a few other hotels, thinking maybe details had gotten blurred given the circumstances. Nope. They were nowhere to be found at any of the surrounding hotels by the name they gave us. So Danielle and I drove on home that night without her cell phone.

When people asked me about our hike, and I told the story of the Canadian couple and leaving the cell phone, I got some interesting reactions from a few folks—a life lesson for myself. I was stopped in my tracks more than once when telling the story. One person even said, "I would have never left my cell phone. I paid way too much for my phone." Hmm . . . imagine that! Dollar bills fogging out kindness.

The next day I stayed cooped up in my home office, organizing GoPro footage and still shots while making notes about our day. Around nine thirty that morning, I was reflecting on some previous notes and came across Caitlin Moore's name. I put a hold on what I was originally working on and began drafting an email to *Survivor.*

I started off by explaining to Caitlin that my doctor had mentioned to me a few times now to let him know if I wanted another letter written up, for me to send to the show for clearance to give the game another shot. I told her I was still interested in being a competitor on the show and that I hoped to hear back from her soon.

After hitting the "send" button, I sat quietly, still cooped up watching and listening to my past in slow motion. A few hours later a message popped up in my inbox from Caitlin Moore. She said she was thrilled to hear that I was fighting to give *Survivor* another shot and that they would be casting in late October/early November. She ended the message with "We all really like you for the show, and this time around, as long as you are healthy, I'll do everything I can to make it happen!!"

By the end of the week I decided to take a trip to a place that I was definitely a stranger to—the bookstore Barnes & Noble. After having such an uplifting hike on the official Livestrong Day, I decided it was time to go out and purchase Lance Armstrong's book *It's Not About the Bike*. I had no intention of reading his book. But I wanted to have it in my possession. I came home and placed it on my office desk and laid my rosary beads that came from the Holy Land on top of the book and left it be.

Once Danielle saw the book, she said, "Oh, look at that. You bought the book Dr. Lee told you not to read. So that's going to be the first book you ever read?" I answered, "Nope. I bought that book to add to my collection. Having that book right there is going to inspire me. What one man can do, another man can do." Then I added, "Lance Armstrong didn't even write this book, you know. He worked with an author named Sally Jenkins." Danielle asked, "What are you going to do with it?" I paused and said, "I'm going to pick it up every once in a while, flip through the pages, and think about my own story and my own personal journey with cancer. It's going to help me figure out a way to dig deep inside of myself and become the true author of my own life." Danielle smiled and said, "You are strange, my love!"

If anybody can relate to crying like a five-year-old, to the point where tears are flowing over your cheekbones while breathing heavily, this was what began to happen to me on October 7. I looked at Danielle as I wiped my right hand down my face, clearing tears away from my shaggy, growing facial hair, and said in a deep, growling, painful kind of voice, "Look at me, Danielle! Look at what is happening to me. LOOK AT MY FACE!"

This had been the first time in my life that she had ever seen me behave like this. I sat down on two small steps at the end of our back hallway and began taking long, deep breaths, trying to control myself. I then explained to Danielle what was wrong. My father had informed me that he was choosing to put an end to his marriage with my mother after thirty years. I stayed put for some time on those steps and thought about how I had never witnessed my parents fighting or even raising their voices at one another. I grew up listening to a lot of other people speak about my parents as if they had an inspiring relationship.

For me, watching the love between my parents was inspiring. Growing up, I would watch their facial expressions closely; they always seemed to greatly respect one another. My father once told me that he felt like the luckiest guy in the world because he was able to fall in love with my mother over and over again. It was absolutely amazing to witness as a child.

Love and hate are what I observed as time passed in my parents' once-inspiring relationship. I have to believe that observing this kind of transition taught me something important about my own future when it came to relationships and becoming a husband and later a father. My mother and father both started speaking to me on separate terms, venting to me in small doses of negativity about the other person. It never felt like it was my place to elaborate on these kinds of conversations other than listening. I have not been married for thirty years nor have I raised three children. So I continued learning from these two people I loved with all my heart.

What became difficult for me was years of living through the acted-out role of happiness. My parents were like an anchor when it came to holidays or family gatherings. What I wondered at times was, once all the plates and silverware got put away and the company went home, what kind of real emotions were left on the table?

As much disappointment as the news brought me, I am thankful for my parents' masked relationship for strengthening how I handle real situations in my own world. After choosing to share a life with Danielle, I have been able to express myself and be real, allowing us to be free from feeling afraid of one another face to face, even if it seems heart crumbling at times.

A couple of days later, I drove back into Boston to meet with a doctor that I had never met before. His name was Dr. Fernandez, and he specialized in speaking to cancer patients as a therapist. I have always been against speaking to a therapist. I had canceled my appointment with him twice already because of my feelings about sharing details in my life with somebody I didn't even know. I was going to call the night before and cancel for the third time, but after the built-up emotions I was feeling, I figured what the hell. I would go see what talking to a therapist was like.

On my drive into the city, I cranked the radio up, and the first song that came on immediately put a spin on my day: "Live Like You Were Dying" by country superstar Tim McGraw. It was like two strings were tied to each one of my cheeks, yanking them back as I smiled, putting the *J* back in joy as I cruised down the freeway.

There was a short wait in Dr. Fernandez's office, and then my name was called by the doctor himself. He walked me to a small square room with a desk that he took a seat behind, and then he put his hand out and pointed to two seats up against the wall. "Please sit, David." I looked the doctor in the eyes and began fishing around in my zipped-up hoody pocket for my GoPro and said, "Before we start, do you have any problem with me putting this camera on your desk and documenting everything said in this room today?" He looked a little taken aback at first, but he agreed by saying, "I guess so . . ."

I hit the "record" button and then BOOM! I went off like a shaken champagne bottle. I wasn't even sure if I was making any kind of logical sense. After I calmed down, Dr. Fernandez began going over a few questions that he wanted to ask me about how I dealt with my cancer, treatments, and surgeries.

At this turning point in our meeting, I could answer with some comfort. Then once he told me we had run out of time, he opened up his door and walked me out after I swiped the GoPro off his desk. I felt like I had been in a fistfight or something. I was dazed and confused, yet eager to replay my actions that the GoPro captured so I could learn more about what I had put myself through mentally.

One thing I did learn was that I did not like speaking to a therapist. I felt worse deep down inside after spilling out all kinds of confused emotions to some guy I didn't know from a hole in the wall. I realized, after being stuck in that one-hour-long storm of a conversation, that I was better off lying down somewhere that suited me best, taking a few deep breaths, and trying to ask myself the correct questions and then working even harder on answering them honestly at a pace that allowed me to feel good about me.

Later that night after dinner, I walked to the end of the driveway to get the mail. There was a small package with a Canadian address on the top-left corner. Sure enough, it was Danielle's cell phone. There was also a thank-you card. A few folded-up bills slid out of the card and onto the table as I opened it. The card read, "I could never thank you enough, but that won't keep me from trying." Then in cursive writing with a black pen, it read, "Danielle, thank you sooo much for the use of your cell phone. My husband and I are so grateful for your act of generosity and kindness. You saved our lives. Laure and YUs xx." Then on the bottom-right side of the card, it read, "We left a little bit of money to cover the calls." I spread out the folded-up bills that fell onto the table, and there were four American twenty-dollar bills!

Good, kindhearted people do exist.

The first place my mind went after reading this thank-you card was directly to the conversation I had with the individual that said, "I would have never left my cell phone. I paid way too much for my phone." The lesson I learned that day was knowing who I wouldn't want wandering by if I had stumbled and fallen and needed help.

Another forty-eight hours later, I was about to get a brand new shock in my life. My father stood in front of his three children, tongue-tied with tears brimming in his eyes, as the words "I tried to commit suicide" stuttered out of his mouth.

Immediately I thought back to passing conversations I'd witnessed when someone had mentioned suicide in my father's presence. He would always say, "How do you fail at trying to kill yourself?" and "What kind of person talks about trying to kill himself or herself? If you're gonna do it,

THEN DO IT."

My father stood there, stone cold as ever, after he dropped the word *suicide*. I watched his glassy eyes bounce back and forth in his head as he paced around the room. I stayed silent and observed his actions for a few seconds until he came to a standstill and went wide eyed without even a blink, looking my way. My two sisters stood beside me, speechless.

There were few words exchanged between my father, my two sisters, and myself in the remaining minutes before I nodded and walked out the door. The ride home was when some heavy confusion started to sink into my brain. I began to wonder why my father was even able to tell me that he had tried to commit suicide. I was curious as to why a man that did everything he said he was going to do had failed at something he aggressively looked down on others for doing.

It would be accurate to say that I was spinning into a world of anger. I was truly starting to believe that I was disconnected from reality. I only had about two and a half months left to continue documenting my journey through 2012, and I was lost at that moment. Misdirected. I wasn't even sure if this inspiration project I had set out to create would have a positive ending!

The next morning, on October 12, I lay in my bed like I did when I returned home after my second and third cycles of chemotherapy, feeling polluted, diluted, mentally disturbed, warped, and burnt out, trying to spin a negative into a positive.

Thoughts even crossed my mind during this fucked-up case of temporary depression about teaching my father a lesson by having his son show him how to kill himself. That would put an end to the project; that would wrap up documenting a real-life story about survival with a twist while teaching somebody a life lesson by sacrificing another. But I knew this was wrong, and I couldn't even believe where my head had gone at this given point in my life. I was so full of disturbed anger intertwined with confusion that I was beginning to draw a blank to all humanity.

I decided it was time for a serious physical and mental reset. I called up Shane Wakeen to see if he was up for a day on Mount Washington. He said, "Weren't you up there the other day?" I replied, "Yes, I was. I heard they got fresh snow." Shane said he was in. I hung up the phone pretty stoked, knowing I would be back in an environment where I could regain my composure, which I knew would help me be able to put that spin back on turning a negative frame of mind into a positive, allowing life to become an inspiration again.

***When demons begin mumbling,
I embrace a place where angels whisper.***

It was an exceptional day the next morning in the White Mountains. The weather had consisted of all four seasons that New England had to offer here on the East Coast. The hike started off with an early springlike warmth in the air, and all low-growing vegetation was full and alive with a plush-green coloring throughout the trail. The sun shined as bright as summer, casting down beautiful rays of light past scattered treetops into crystal-clear trickling brooks and running streams that cut through the earth. Rushing waterfalls flowed, and vibrant green moss lined rocky edges along the wetlands.

The landscape began to make a slow transition to autumn. Bright yellow leaves still held on tight to birch trees, and the low aliveness of plush-green growth started to fade into a yellowish brown as temperatures dropped, making any fallen leaves below our feet brittle. We continued to crunch our way step by step up a trail named Boot's Spur.

After walking through what was now a landscape full of bare hardwoods, with all their leaves curled up dead and scattered below the treetops, our eyes started to witness the season of winter moving in, even though it was still officially fall in New Hampshire. The leafless trees stayed to our back side as the mountain began to fill up with a thick cluster of evergreens covered in fresh white snow, creating a winter wonderland only hours into the hike.

I was snapping photographs like somebody was going to be paying me for the prints. Every time my eye looked through the lens, I saw an award-winning photo and nothing else. Shane and I looked at one another at one point and started talking about how incredible the visuals were today.

It didn't take much time at all to truly embrace where I was on that day, on October 13. The negative mumbling in my head was smothered out as an uplifting whisper began clearing my mind of anything that may have been bothering me the last few days. I was experiencing life that had been here way before my time and will remain changing, season after season, leaving behind the same outcome over and over again. **Beauty—real, rugged beauty—is what will remain in the White Mountains.**

I came home from that hike feeling like I was on a new level. Mother Nature had once again proven herself to be the best remedy! My cell phone started ringing after I stepped out of a long, hot shower. It was my mother in a worked-up, tearful voice. I asked, "What is wrong?" She replied, "Your father has been admitted into a psychiatric hospital." I told her, "Clearly, he is losing control of all his emotions. Maybe he can't seem to bear the hurt he sees you going through, based on his decisions. He's spinning out of control, Mom. I'm not sure what we can do to help." After a couple long, deep breaths, I thanked my mother for the call and told her I loved her. I gently hung up the phone and explained to Danielle what the call was all about and then made the decision to stay tuned into what I was about to do next, which was drift off to a place of meditative sleep. That was how I chose to handle that kind of news.

The next week felt like a great storm of chaos had moved into the forecast. On Monday, October 15, I got a call from my uncle

Peter, asking if he could stop by to drop off a few things. Once he got to my home, he started unpacking his truck with firearms that had belonged to my father. My father had asked him to take the weapons off his hands after being admitted into the hospital seeking mental health help. My uncle asked if I could keep them locked up in my safe for the time being. Before my uncle drove away, he asked me how I was doing. I told him I felt like I was not even living in reality anymore. He closed his eyes slowly and sighed, saying, "That's the thing, David. This is reality; it's all real."

I spent the rest of my weekdays that week climbing trees and running my crane on different jobs that I had previously booked. I shut my phone off after each job was completed. Going home and cherishing the love I felt for Danielle, Ava D., and Kiana was what kept me balanced, stable, and level headed during the intense adrenaline rush of reality that I pushed into a place I couldn't even seem to describe.

By midweek I started to think about my father sitting inside of a mental hospital and then about my mother and how she might be handling each night all by herself. After Ava D. and Kiana went to sleep for the night, I walked into my office and scooped up my rosary beads and told Danielle I was going for a ride to my mother's. Once I pulled in the driveway, I saw that all the lights were off. I walked into the house and called out "Mom" a few times as I walked around. No answer. I walked into her room, and the bedroom light was dim, but my mother was not home.

I walked over to her nightstand and saw a large book beside the bed with a pair of reading glasses sitting on top of it. It was the Holy Bible. I picked up the book and placed it on her side of the bed next to her pillow and then took off my rosary beads and laid them on top of the Bible. Then I grabbed a small note pad and pen that I saw on the nightstand and wrote out a message to my mother. "Mom, please take these rosary beads as a gift and hold on to them for strength. I can't even explain the kind of strength I have found when I drape these around my neck. I hope you can find the same kind of strength as I have. I love you. David." Then I tucked the piece of paper under the cross and made my way back home.

Ending the week off on Friday, October 19, Danielle and I drove back up north to spend the next two nights in the White Mountains, attending a wedding in which Danielle was going to be a bridesmaid. Her first cousin Amy Roberge was getting married at the National Historic Landmark in New England, the Mount Washington Grand Hotel.

I spent the next few hours roaming all of this grand piece of property, taking photographs and filming. I even spent some time taking photos of my historic suite from the outside of the building so I could remember where I was. This stick-built monster of a dwelling was made of fancy crown moldings, colossal columns, fine rugs, and some cool vintage elevators, all built on American soil by a New Hampshire entrepreneur named Joseph Stickney. Over two years Stickney and his crew had pieced together what was known as a Spanish renaissance revival estate in Bretton Woods, New Hampshire, completed in 1902. It had been designed to accommodate a generation of American kings, and that's exactly what I felt like on that night, sitting around a circular table with Danielle's uncles, aunts, cousins, and family and friends, munching on some grub, sucking down alcoholic beverages, and shooting the breeze with good company during the rehearsal dinner.

The next morning I woke slowly as the sunrise pierced through our room windows. Danielle's warm upper body lifted off of my chest. She gave me a kiss on my forehead and climbed out of the bed, gently stepping her naked body into the bathroom. I lay there staring at the ceiling, thinking about what I was going to do with my time today. Danielle was spending the day with her cousin, Amy, and the wedding party, getting ready for the night's celebration.

After showering, getting dressed, and filling up on some breakfast, I went on a morning nature walk with my in-laws. The trail we took brought me out to a pretty awesome memory—a place that I had not been in over a decade. We ended up at a watering hole called Ammonoosuc Upper Falls, where I had spent a lot of my time diving off cliffs during my teenage years with friends and family. There was a white birch tree still standing that grew out of the highest rock that some people used to climb for extra height before making the plunge into ice-cold mountain water.

On our way back to the hotel, we passed a few folks horseback riding, and then the trail opened up to the front of a plush-green golf course. As we made our way closer to the hotel, I noticed people dining on an outdoor patio and couldn't wait to pull up a seat and have some lunch. I dined solo as I gazed out at Mount Washington.

I overheard somebody dining beside me say that the view looked like a painting, which it did. It was grand and gorgeous and created by Mother Nature. I smiled because I felt like part of me was sitting in this mid-October portrait of Mount Washington this year.

I had learned earlier in the day that Native American tribes referred to this grand mountain as Agiocochook. The past few weekends hiking up and down this breathtaking portrait had brought me back to a moment where Danielle and I had pulled off the trail to take a break during our hike. I had snapped a shot of the hotel I was now having lunch at. We were so high up that you could hold your thumb out in front of your face, close one eye, and make the whole place disappear.

I had turned to Danielle and said, "It won't be long until we are celebrating Amy and Justin's marriage under that red roof way down there, Danielle!" Then over a week later Shane and I roamed all over that mountain with its powder-coated peak and with fresh white snow under our feet. Then a week after that, I'm wolfing down a cheeseburger on the outdoor patio of the hotel, thinking back to where I had snapped that photo with Danielle and realizing that today the artist didn't use a speck of white in her artwork that I was gazing deep into!

The night of Amy and Justin's wedding, on October 20, was one for the books. Danielle and I ate more good food, got drunk, and danced like nobody was watching all the way off the dance floor and into the hotel lobby. Danielle and I stood there waiting for one of the old vintage elevators to give us a ride to our floor so we could enjoy our romantic, historic suite. We gazed intensely into each other's eyes, thinking about what was only an elevator ride away.

We decided to scratch the elevator and walked and danced down the halls. Danielle was singing and laughing up the stairwell, passing by each closed door until we spotted our room number. We practically busted the door down to our suite.

The lighting was dim, with a lit fireplace casting a flickering glow all throughout the room. I turned on the radio to whatever station came in clear, and it quickly became background noise. This fiery, glowing suite became a heaven of pure pleasure.

The night ended with a hot shower and room service. Then we turned off the lights, and we both slid under the sheets. Once we were both settled under the covers, I pressed my lips hard into her lips and said, "I love you, Danielle."

It felt amazing to be able to connect intimately with Danielle again. Since the chemotherapy had been flowing through my bloodstream, Danielle had stayed clear of me due to the toxins that my body was capable of releasing, not only for her safety but most of all because she was still breastfeeding Kiana during my treatments. Then after seven weeks of focusing on flushing out my entire body for good of chemo, I spent a few months healing up from my stomach surgery. So this was the first night that I had not felt contaminated or injured and could finally love my wife with passion again.

On Monday, October 22, I began my day with a drive back toward Boston's Mass General. I'd be getting my scans and blood work taken to make sure that I was truly done with chemotherapy, knives, and scalpels. Halfway through my scans, I shot up and reached for the trash bin near the wall and vomited. First time that had ever happened. I remember walking into the waiting room thinking to myself how I had one clean scan after my first surgery, and the second scan was actually the one that sent me for a loop. I was worked up about being under surveillance today, not knowing what the future could bring. All I knew was that I wanted clean results putting an end to cancer.

To get through the next week of waiting for my results, I booked myself solid with crane work, tree work, and firewood deliveries. Seven days later, Danielle and I wrapped up October with a drive into Boston. We both took a seat and waited for the doctor with a bow tie to arrive and give us my surveillance results since the vomiting scan. When Dr. Lee entered the room, he exuded positive energy and immediately presented the news that put Mass General and CANCER in our rearview mirror. Danielle and I thanked him and left the hospital for good, headed northbound back home to our girls.

That night before bed, I grabbed my camera and walked to the back of our home. I opened the door to a run-down fourth bedroom in our old farmhouse. There was stuff scattered everywhere: a beat-up twin bed with a plaid cover, a matching dresser in the corner, wet suits laid out on the bed, firearms and gun cases, a guitar, a ukulele, and a longbow on top of the bedcover. On the ground were hunting clothes, sleeping bags, an old car-seat base, folded blankets, and two red mesh bags filled with scuba-diving gear. My favorite piece in this particular room was a five- by four- by three-foot double-doored vintage Protectall safe, which sat next to a window that looked out at the pond and the winter sunset. I stood there in the doorway and thought to myself, "This is it . . . This is going to be the writing room. A place for me to learn how to read and write on my own terms while making art out of my own life."

November, or rather Movember the official mustache month, had arrived, with only six workdays booked on the calendar. Marking up calendars was something I had been doing for years. When I was young, my father would always say keep a calendar book around and make a note at the end of each day. He would challenge me to see if I could do it for an entire year.

Work or play—make a note for your day!

I had been doing this for years, and the best part of each year was to reflect back and see what had happened. This year's calendar was definitely going to be one I would never forget.

I booked work for Monday and Tuesday, then had two days off, and then back to work on Friday. Trees got climbed, pruned, and felled. I drove around southern New Hampshire, delivering firewood to different residents. The Micmac crane picked things up and put them down, and the homeowners were happy, money got deposited in the bank, and help was paid. A lot of my energy and time shifted on my days off. I cooked meals for my family, laughed, and played. I gave Ava D. and Kiana baths, changed diapers, scrubbed their tiny little tusks, and listened to them giggle all the way up the stairs until they were in their pajamas. Life was back and it felt good!

Life was also a topic I wanted to discuss with my father after my workday on Tuesday. It was the first time I had seen or talked with him since he got out of the hospital. I asked him, "Why do you think you ended up in there?" He replied, "I'm not doing good, David." I asked, "Is it because you are having a hard time stepping away from your relationship with Mom after a thirty-year marriage?" He said, "That's part of it. It also has a lot to do with how aggressively I've preached over the years to not only you but the entire family about staying loyal no matter what. I'm also frightened about how my relationship is going to end up with my children."

I looked at my father and said, "Dad, so things are different now, that's all. You're on a new path, starting fresh, which we both know is never easy. Maybe you're not happy with some of the things you have done, said, or even the way you may have handled certain situations with this kind of change in your life. But you're still an inspiring person; you say what you want and do what you want, and people look up to that kind of behavior, and it sounds to me like you're trying to seek happiness, and that's what matters most."

I continued, saying, "I have not been around for that long but long enough to have had my share of listening to married couples that are younger, the same age, and many that are older than me bitch and complain about their loved ones. It may be the one thing in life that will keep me wondering forever—why the person that enjoys sharing their misery sticks it out. Then I think even deeper during one of these kinds of conversations about the other person in the relationship that chooses not to share their misery with others. It's the saddest thing in the whole damn world. Misery enjoys company. So please, do me and yourself a favor and don't end up like that. To me, those kind of people seem to be the weakest of the weak."

My father looked at me with another stone-cold look on his face and said, "Thank you so much for understanding; you are a wonderful man, David."

I smirked at my father and said, "I'm surprised you're even out of that mental hospital. I think if I was in your shoes, I'd still be in there, sipping on a fruit cup or something." I got him to crack a smile and even laugh a little bit, and then I said one more time, **"You're on a new path, Dad. Go for it!"**

Once I got in my truck and drove away, I began to realize how much deep-down anger I really had about this dramatic real-life family crisis, which somehow seemed to hit me harder than hearing the word *cancer* for the first time back in 2011. I guess after looking up to a man that had become a role model to me and preached for years and years about that word *loyalty*, it had truly twisted me up emotionally. The only reason I believe I was even able to stand in front of my father and speak to him in a positive way, in a controlled discussion face to face, was that happiness will always outweigh misery. So I tucked my anger away and let the real side of me shine through during our talk, which ultimately cheered him on about pursuing happiness!

During the first full week of November, Danielle and I cranked up the radio and got busy each night after the girls went to sleep. The job was to turn a third bedroom in our old farmhouse into an art piece and playroom. After clearing out miscellaneous things that had been tossed in there over the past few years, we created a clean blank canvas for us to look at. Danielle said proudly, "Let's go with bright outdoor colors!"

We made a family trip to the local hardware store ten minutes down the road. We needed a new electric box, covers, and switches, as well as cans of bright-colored paints, different-sized brushes, and rollers for our project. At the end of Friday night, Danielle and I looked at each other and nodded our heads, proud at what we had accomplished. Each ceiling fan blade had been painted yellow with orange streaks of paint, made by dipping a wild turkey feather into the paint, to mimic the sun. Three of the four walls were green with one wall painted blue. The blue wall had two windows in the middle of it, with red, orange, yellow, green, blue, and purple stripes giving a rainbow effect in the left corner of the room. The ceiling was painted a light blue with large cumulus clouds scattered above that Danielle painted by using a big sponge used for washing the cars. This art piece came out top-notch, sending out a vibe of cheerfulness in our home.

After cleaning up all the painting stuff, I booted up the laptop. It had been a while since I checked my emails. I scanned through mostly junk and then my eyes spotted news from *Survivor.*

"Hi David! Attached is a packet for potential contestants for *Survivor* 27/28. I've attached the S27/28 application as well. This must be returned in order to be considered for our finals, which will take place from December 7 through 14. I cannot pitch you for the finals without this packet being returned in advance of the pitch. There are detailed rules inside the packet to help you complete the forms. Please be advised, I will need all immediate family releases as well. Cheers, Caitlin."

I was asked to create another three-minute video. The casting department wanted me to talk about what I had been going through over the past eight to nine months. It was a humbling email to read, knowing that *Survivor* was still thinking about giving me another shot. Over the next twenty-four hours, I thought about how I was even going to put together a new casting video.

Stress was flowing through my body by Sunday. Caitlin Moore had asked for the new footage to be back in her hands in a few days. The application wasn't due back until November 20. I needed to clear my mind and get focused this morning. I chose manual labor to try to help with this task. I headed out into the backyard with a spade shovel in one hand and a steel rake in another to clean out an overflow brook to the pond so that high rainwater would drain with ease. I was having a hard time brainstorming about how to compact the last eight to nine months into a three-minute clip.

After raking and shoveling leaves into an old compost that had built up in the brook, I pulled the GoPro from my front pants pocket and sat up against a dry-stacked stone wall with tall brownish ornamental grasses in the backdrop. I began speaking into the eye of the GoPro. I tried to link some of my experiences to *Survivor*, but after filming four clips, I put the GoPro back in my pants pocket and thought about sending in the first take. I was having a lot of trouble explaining my past year in one sitting.

Later that night I shared with Danielle the footage I was going to send *Survivor*. She looked at me and started laughing. I said, "I'm not coming across like myself at all, huh? I'm not making any sense right now. I think it's because I am still in the middle of creating my own survivor project, which has a deadline of December 31, 2012." I paused and then said, "How am I going to explain what I have been through if it's not even over yet? I really don't even want to play the game or be part of a reality TV show at all anymore, but I think it might be in my best interest, for some reason." Danielle replied, "You do what you gotta do, Dave."

I spent the following Monday and Tuesday relaxing. I was a homebody for the next forty-eight hours, chilling on the front porch, working in the yard, playing with my children, and spending time with Danielle. Tuesday night I decided to finally send *Survivor* an email with my new casting video attached, not really feeling all that great about the new content I had put together.

The next day I heard some interesting news through the grapevine about the world's most famous cancer survivor. Lance Armstrong had announced he was a phony baloney! Later that night, when Danielle got home from work, she said, "David, did you hear about Lance Armstrong?" I said, "I sure did!" I walked into the office, picked up his book, and came walking into the kitchen, saying with authority, "What one man can do, another man can do! This book is full of lies in every library or bookshelf it sits in, Danielle, and he didn't even write it himself. The most famous cancer survivor ever may end up being the most famous liar in sports history."

I'm aware I don't have the right to judge anybody who walks on the face of this earth. I'm also aware that Lance Armstrong is the face of a cause that has helped millions of people and families push through a life-threatening disease called cancer, in a positive, uplifting way. I tip my hat in his direction while wondering one thing about this person I don't even know, who had become an inspiration to me during my own battle with cancer. Is he still living strong?

On Thursday, November 15, I fired up my crane for a local tree service, renting out my rig and myself as the operator for the day. This was one of the most amusing learning experiences I have had as a crane operator. I watched the boss of the company scream like a fool at each one of the employees all morning long. Every once in a while, one of the workers would walk up to the side of the crane and say to me, "I fucking hate this guy" or "This guy doesn't know how to treat people." The boss even came up to the side of the crane and said, "None of these guys know what the fuck they're doing. They're all stupid as fuck."

Each person on the job kept doing this all day long. It stayed in a rotation. I couldn't even believe how intense it had gotten. It was like they were waiting their turn to come talk with me. It's amazing how much we can learn from watching a team of people in any kind of trade or business, whether they wear a white, blue, or pink collar, who don't get along with one another. Especially when the leader chooses to act like a stupid fuck. A working environment is built up of many parts, and when the foundation is out of line, it becomes a disaster and never finishes correctly no matter what the job title is.

Friday night Danielle and I drove back into Boston. Not to sit and talk with doctors but for a night out at a dance club with Mr. and Mrs. Wakeen. This was when I first realized how much of an impact Movember was actually making by the reaction I got from rocking a mustache for men's health awareness. There were high fives and comments thrown in the air by people I didn't even know all night long. There was some serious attention drawn to facial hair for sure in the city that night.

Saturday morning I woke up early, ready to hunt! After a fifteen-minute truck ride, I pulled up beside a big old yellow farmhouse, built back in the 1800s, and then rolled up slowly beside my cousin Bill "the Bull" Murray. We geared up and loaded the shotguns for an early hunt. After walking past some overgrown apple trees, Bill bore to the right into a cornfield. I went low and left through the cornfield toward some wetlands. It was a long, slow, quiet walk near the water's edge, spooking beavers into the stream as small branches snapped under my feet, walking upstream.

I stalked for about three hundred yards and climbed into an old tree stand I had set up in a double maple years ago. Beavers had owned this area of the woods. About every twenty minutes to a half hour, one would swim by, making a wake of ripples with the top of its head and eyeballs sticking above the water level. Squirrels were running around going nuts; small birds chirped continuously as Canada geese flew overhead.

It was a great morning to be in the woods. I was covered up with an orange-fleece cowboy hat, an old saddlecloth zip-up hoodie, and a pair of cargo pants that had a faded-out Mossy Oak break-up pattern. The bottoms of my pants were tucked into some tall Lacrosse rubber boots, and I had on a pair of Mossy Oak shooting gloves with a Remington twelve-gauge pump-action shotgun in my hands, waiting patiently for a white-tailed deer to walk on by and get in shooting range.

I was hoping to get a deer hunt on camera, but that did not happen this morning. Part of my problem spending time in the woods hunting this year was me and my GoPro. I kept taking the GoPro out and talking into it, sharing ideas and thoughts that were on my mind. I'm not sure if there is a hunter in history that can go into the wild, have full-out conversations up in a tree, and still have wildlife mosey on by. So deer hunting had mostly become a place for me to sit and brainstorm out loud.

Sunday, November 18, was a pretty big deal. I curled my mustache up with wax, put on a red-and-black lumberjack button-down shirt and clean jeans, and lit the wood stoves in preparation for Danielle and I hosting all our immediate family members on both sides to celebrate Kiana's one-year-old birthday party. It was amazing sitting at the dining room table, watching my baby girl stuff her face with handfuls of cake after her big sister helped her blow out the single flickering flame on the number-one candle.

After Danielle and I cleaned up our home and our company had left for the night, we plopped down on the couch in front of the wood stove and started having a conversation about how chaotic and hectic Kiana's first year had been and how she and Ava D. would never even remember this year.

I explained to Danielle that part of my drive during this

obsessive filming journey started to revolve around Ava D. and Kiana. Every day so far during 2012 had been such a valuable learning experience, and I was excited to one day be able to share what I had documented with others.

The one thing in life I have never had a fear of is death. I am well aware there will be a day when my name and photograph will end up in an obituary. So I wanted to have something tangible and timeless like a book expressing and articulating myself in a way that would be available if my children ever wanted to learn about their pops. **It would forever be available with raw honesty** about my feelings toward not only them but the love that I truly had for their mother during a special chapter in my life.

November 20 was the day my second *Survivor* application was due back to Caitlin Moore. So the game was on my mind before I headed out the door to spend the day feeling free and at peace while climbing around in white oaks and poplar trees with the last lumberjack still kicking around my side. I called him Slim Jim. He was born and raised as an axeman in Canada. According to Jim, his father used to start his chainsaw because he started running a chainsaw so young that he couldn't even fire one up by himself. Jim was about forty-five years old, six feet, and 140 pounds with a full, thick head of hair and a matching mustache above a mouth that had a few missing teeth in his smile. He was one of the happiest-go-lucky guys around town. I've known Slim Jim since I was twelve years old, and he has become one of my best friends in the tree industry.

Once I returned home from work, Danielle asked me if I was going to pursue the second shot I might have with *Survivor*. She said, "Wasn't your paperwork due back today?" I answered, "Yes, it was." She said, "Did you ever mail your packet back." I said,

"Not yet, I didn't." She looked puzzled and said, "Didn't you say that it was due today?" I said, "Yes, I did, but I have not made up my mind completely, and maybe it's too late. I really don't know what the hell I am doing when it comes to *Survivor*." Danielle smiled and walked past me.

I walked into the barn and reached down into the firewood bin and took out a handful of kindling. I grabbed a blowtorch off my workbench on my way back in. Some cold weather had moved in quickly so I was going to fire up the kitchen wood stove for the first time this year to take the chill out of the air before we all sat down for dinner.

Danielle came walking into the kitchen and said, "What are you doing now? Why do you feel the need to take pictures of yourself making a fire?" I had the GoPro set up on a tripod in front of the wood stove with the Nikon camera in my hand, snapping shots of the burning flames inside of the stove. I told Danielle that this was an important fire. It was the first time using this wood stove this year, and I wanted to document what I was using to warm up our home. "What are you using?" she asked. "I'm feeding the stove my application from *Survivor*." By this time, Danielle was in the next room, and she popped her head around the corner and looked down at me and said,

"Why?"

"You know, I'm a strong believer in 'everything happens for a reason.' There's gotta be a good reason for why I got knocked down as hard as I did before stepping foot in the game and possibly being able to commit in that direction the first time around.

I'm not sure if I will ever know if what I'm choosing to do is correct or not. But I am making a decision. Caitlin explained that if I did make it on the show, I would be away playing the game for forty days straight, right? While I have lived through my own real-life survival, and it's been going on a lot longer than forty days and has not even come to an end yet, I still hold immunity in my eyes."

"What changed your mind?" she asked.

"To be honest, Danielle, after putting a hold on my fast-paced work life back in March during chemo, I started to realize how important watching my young growing family really was. Kiana turned one year old the other day. If I had still been working fifteen-hour days and then had stepped away from that overloaded workaholic lifestyle and actually made it on *Survivor*, stepping away from a world that was blocking the three of you out in the first place by filling it with forty days on some remote island without communication, I can't even image what it would have been like giving up the memories that I have been able to share and cherish with you and our girls the past nine months.

"I know that it has not been easy watching me go through treatment, surgeries, and career changes, but I've been able to experience moments with my children that I will never get to recreate, and I wouldn't trade that for the world."

I stoked the fire in the stove and watched my *Survivor* application slowly burn away.

Thanksgiving Day was here! A day to count all our blessings and be thankful for everything life had to offer. For me, it marked the year I was thankful to have two daughters, a wife that adored life, a roof over my family's head, warm beds to lie in, a fridge and freezer full of food, a father who chose to embrace his life instead of ending it, and most of all to be cancer-free.

Chapter Eight

Focused on the Prize

On the morning of December 1, 2012, I tossed on a soft light gray bathrobe and walked my tired, worn-out body straight into my office, where I grabbed a pen and wrote out the word "INSPIRATIONAL" on the calendar, above the month of December.

The next day I was up bright and early, ready to spend my morning in the woods to give it one more shot at capturing a white-tailed-deer hunt on camera. There was a thin coat of fresh snow on the ground so tracking was going to be a little easier today. I bundled up in camo, packed myself up with ammo, and headed out back behind my home for a morning hunt.

As soon as I passed the pond, there were some fresh single tracks in the snow from a smaller-sized white-tail. The tracks went on for about fifty yards or so, heading to the edge of some large pine trees. The tracks stopped at an oval-shaped wet spot on the ground where all the snow was melted; it was clear the deer had bedded down for a bit. Then the tracks picked back up and crossed over an old stone wall in the woods. I began following the tracks slowly and then heard some crunching footsteps nearby. I paused for a moment and then heard the sound of four dashing footsteps in the distance. I thought to myself, "Damn! I blew it."

I quickly tucked myself into an old, fallen pine treetop to use as a ground blind facing the old stone wall, hoping that if I sat quietly and patiently, the deer would circle back around, allowing me to fire a shot off. About a half hour had passed, and a thought ran through my mind, so I turned on the GoPro to quietly document it.

I was thinking a lot about what Diane Sollars had said to me a few months back at my older sister's engagement party. She said, "David, tell your story, and let it inspire others, and take care of you and your family for the rest of your life." It was a powerful statement, and her wise words had been marinating in my mind ever since. **I finally realized that this project I had set out to create was going to be a success, but only if I finished it.**

The completion of something I'd started that had been designed to hopefully inspire myself and others along the way was going to be the ultimate success. I knew there was a long, rough road ahead before that feeling even entered my life. But like any kind of goal that we set and conquer, the first feeling of success would always be self-gratification. Then when the vision grows larger, the passion, honesty, and hard work have the ability to take over the entire process, which then enables nature to take its course.

So sitting up against an old, dead pine treetop with a twelve-gauge in my hands, reflecting back on Diane's wise words, it all finally started making some sense. If I reached that feeling of self-gratification on this project, then I could love myself for who I really was deep down inside. Then with that kind of internal self-respect, I would be able to take care of my family correctly for the rest of my life.

Shortly after I shut off the GoPro, I spotted some movement about forty yards away, directly in front of me. I tucked the shotgun's wooden stock into my shoulder and looked through the scope to focus in on a brown body slowly moving through some large red oak trees and a lot of thick underbrush. The brown body began moving farther away from me as I slowly lost sight of it. Then the deer's tail went straight up in the air, showing all the white fur on its backside, which caught my attention immediately. I tucked the stock back into my shoulder and watched the white-tail bound away with freedom through some large, thick red oaks.

This hunt was going to be my last one during the New Hampshire 2012 hunting season. I thought for sure I was going to put down a white-tail on camera this year, but I did not, and I counted my blessings for grocery stores. **Even a poor hunter can eat good these days.**

Later that afternoon my family and I roamed all around a

Christmas tree farm, looking for the right one to cut down. Once we spotted the correct evergreen for our home, I knelt down and began sawing away with Ava D. and Kiana staring down, watching closely. I yelled out "TIMBER" as the tree slowly fell to the ground, and a smile grew on Ava D.'s face. After we hauled the tree away, the girls got hot cocoa and cookies inside a small barn on the property. Then, when we returned back to our home, I dragged the tree into our living room, and it all seemed like the craziest tradition to do every single year. Once the tree was standing in place, I decided to prune it with some rose clippers. Basically I baby proofed it so Kiana couldn't reach up and pull on the branches. We decorated the tree with white lights and ornaments for the upcoming holiday. It was the funniest-looking tree we ever had; the branches didn't start until about three feet off the ground. It was the right height for Kiana to walk right underneath with head clearance!

December 3 was the only workday noted on my calendar for the week. It was a full day of crane work, and then after that, my work boots weren't getting laced back up for close to three weeks. I lost track of the days after parking my rig on the third; I wasn't even worried about what time of day it was anymore. It made me remember a question on my *Survivor* application that I had filled out close to a year ago: "Describe what a perfect day would be to you." I answered with "To me, it would be waking up with no alarm clock on vacation in a place where time and even the days of the week are irrelevant."

Once the second week of December rolled around, it was time to capitalize on the question and make it become a reality. On Tuesday morning I looked back on the calendar and circled the number one with a red permanent marker. Since the start of the month I had been looking at life from an interesting angle because one year ago I had fallen from that spruce tree, and when I hit the ground, my entire life spun out of control with good, evil, joy, anger, peace, jealousy, love, greed, hope, resentment, humility, inferiority, kindness, lies, empathy, ego, and truth.

Each day had been part of a learning curve that had put so many things in my own personal life in perspective, which I will never forget. I always seemed to have the pedal pushed to the metal, blurring out views that mattered the most. It was the window of thinking time that I had created in my life that I became grateful for. I felt like I was still in the fast lane, but lately it seemed like the entire world was coming at me in slow motion with the most beautiful view, no matter what direction my eyes wandered in, and it felt really good!

What was rewarding about circling December 1 was that I could finally see the finish line in the distance, and it felt damn good to hold my head up high as I followed my heart while no longer feeling words like evil, anger, jealousy, greed, resentment, inferiority, lies, and most of all ego!

After I drew that red circle around the number one, I also circled the dates for December 12, 13, 14, 15, 16, and 17. Then I packed up the car full of my family's luggage and ended up in Boston at Logan International Airport. Ava D. got shoulder rides all through the airport, and she was the cutest little thing when customs asked her to remove her shoes. She looked up at her mommy with a confused facial expression. Danielle and I started laughing, and then Danielle helped her remove her shoes and place them on a conveyor belt. Once we boarded the aircraft and found our seats, I put my head back and entered relaxation mode en route to Bermuda.

The next seven days were going to be spent on vacation with our cell phones off, waking up with no alarm clock in the background, enjoying tropical blue ocean water with our feet in soft white sand on the beach, letting time and days of the week seem endless.

When we first arrived in Bermuda, the lady at the front desk told us that we were going to have a quiet time here at the resort. She said this week was the slowest they had ever seen since they had been in business. It sounded like it was going to be a good time right from the start.

We jumped on to all different kinds of buses and ferries to explore the island as much as we could, with our days free from alarm clocks and calendars. It was also a time where I could sit in peace and watch Danielle play with our babies, which I believe is a sight that keeps a man hungry to do well in life.

Kiana was still new to walking so she wobbled herself around the beach, pointing at everything she saw and eating sand whenever she could get ahold of it before Danielle or I could stop her. We all went for kayak and paddleboard rides each day we spent at the beach. I decided to grab a mask and snorkel from the desk and wade out to a small sunken wreck about forty-five yards off the beach, and I spotted a zebra nudibranch, which is a sea snail that has no shell and is both male and female all in one. It was a strange yet magnificent little sea creature. Its markings were incredible: vibrant purplish blues with orange coloring on the body and solid dark-purple horns on its head.

Later that afternoon we took a bus ride to the local aquarium. When we arrived, the sign said "Closed" on the door; we were twenty minutes too late. Ava D. had a hard time understanding why we couldn't go into the aquarium. Once we began walking away from the closed door, a young man spoke out and said, "Hey there! Are you guys here to see the aquarium?" I answered, "Yes, that was our plan." He said, "Sorry, we are closed." Then he quickly changed his mind and said, "Come on in. I will give you all a private tour!" **Nothing like seeing a smiling three-year-old who thought she wasn't getting to see the fishies.**

The highlight of the week was a game Ava D. and I came up with called Towel Twister. I spun up a beach towel, put it around her back, and then brought both ends up under her armpits and twisted the two ends together so I could pick her up with the towel. Then she and I began spinning round and round until down looked like up, and up looked like down. It was a great time all week long, spending time with my family. Bermuda was so much more than we had expected, and we would definitely go back. On December 17 we packed up our bags and made our way through customs back into the United States.

Two days back home from Bermuda and I woke up with another let's-make-a-deal attitude! I started to replay a few words that got passed around between Dan the Tree Man and myself a while back. He had already bought the bucket truck so I was back in sales mode, trying to brainstorm another deal I could offer him to make him buy what was left of Roy's Tree Service. Hopefully, it would be another deal too good for him to pass up. Dan also told me that he was thinking of buying a crane one day. I quickly responded by saying, "Dan, why don't you wait a bit before you go out and buy one. I'll give you a good deal on this one." He laughed and said, "You're going to sell the crane too!" I told Dan, "After the rest of Roy's equipment is gone, this crane isn't going to be parked at my home for much longer." I laughed out loud. "I have a plan, Dan!" He scratched his head and looked inquisitively at me before walking away.

On the afternoon of December 19, I had another talk with Dan the Tree Man. He and I came to a verbal agreement on the rest of the Roy's Tree Service equipment, and the crane sat on the back burner for the time being.

Later that night I informed Danielle that it was only a matter of time before the tree service was the next source of income to be put out of its misery. I could tell she was a little on edge about my actions, but I had explained to her that I needed to create a larger window of time so I could commit everything, all of me right down to the core, to my project. My vision needed all the attention I could give it for it to come out correctly, and I made it clear that I did not see another way to achieve that. Part of my plan was to keep the crane service around for a little while longer, which gave me the mindset I was looking for moving forward. There would be no more managing employees or spending time driving around southern New Hampshire as a salesman, scraping up tree jobs; it would be me and my crane, and that's it. My hat and gloves were already hung up in the MMA industry while I continued seeking out the simple life.

I contemplated the deal I had made with Dan, not actually knowing what awaited me in the future, but I stuck to my gut feeling and told myself not to FEAR FAILURE. Most of all, I kept reminding myself that **taking big risks meant bigger rewards**.

I reflected back on the past year, and it seemed like it was an interesting year for everyone in the world. I'm not sure if it had anything to do with the hype of 2012 possibly being the end or what the deal was. I was noticing that everybody around me—family, friends, and business acquaintances—was announcing big news, and the general talk among the public seemed to say that this particular year was full of life-changing topics and events. Maybe not though; maybe it's like that every single year, and my eyes had finally opened up to my surroundings a little bit.

Either way, there was a whole lot of marketing spreading worldwide about the world coming to an end in two days' time. A few weeks ago I was sitting at the restaurant Margaritas with my family and Jenni and Shane, talking about the hype of the world coming to an end. Shane started laughing and said, "Look at this," as he picked up a postcard that was at the end of the table. It had a picture of a margarita on it, and the text was advertising for an "End of the World Party" on Friday, December 21. I looked at Shane and said, "Want to go up to the White Mountains on that day and see what Mother Nature has to offer if the world is coming to an end?" Shane smiled and said, "Let's do it!"

I now had plans on December 21, which some might have thought was truly the deadline for life here on Earth. But for myself, I thought it was a bunch of bullshit. December 31, when the clock strikes midnight, was the real deadline in my book, and I was ready to accomplish what I had put my mind to!

On the morning of our hike up the mountain, a huge storm was rolling in, and it was about to hit Agiocochook hard. The day started off with a good, fresh snowfall, but then the sky immediately became calm, and the air warmed up as we continued our drive toward the base of the mountain. The sky was filled with dark and light clouds moving around, changing shapes and designs quickly as our morning continued. Shortly after we started our hike, the sky was covered in thick, dark gray clouds with loud roaring winds as the snow began falling again.

We made it halfway up the Ammonoosuc Ravine Trail and then took a small break. There was a gentleman who was hiking solo that passed us on the trail as we started back up the mountain. It was a quick hello followed by a quick conversation. He had a strong French accent and said he was from Canada.

The weather grew fiercer as we kept moving up in the world. We finally got to a spot where the height of the trees started to get shorter and the forest began slowly disappearing as the high winds picked up speed. The Canadian that had passed us came walking back down the mountain only moments after he had passed us, screaming with excitement, "THE STORM IS RIGHT UP THERE."

After about another seventy yards up the mountain, we came to the Canadian's last foot tracks in the snow. Shane and I looked at each other, nodded our heads, and then agreed it would be best to go another hundred yards past what one person had already seen. We made it to the cascades, which was a little under 4,500 feet. We couldn't even see ten feet in front of us, left, right, up, or down; the conditions had become intense fast.

After fifteen minutes into our decent, all our footprints in the snow were completely covered and blown out from the heavy snowfall and winds, which quickly transitioned into fast-flying ice pellets. The last hour of our hike, the weather made another transition into freezing rain, and temperatures peaked at thirty-two degrees. We ended up back at the truck after a little more than five and a half hours, wearing our snowshoes. The freezing rain continued to fall and then started to turn into rainfall, and then the rain suddenly stopped, and the sky cleared up in the flash of an eye, and it was a beautiful sunset with bright oranges and yellows in the distance, only forty-five minutes into our drive back home.

Later that night, once I fired up the wood stoves, I booted up the computer to check out what kind of weather was recorded on the peak of Mount Washington. The fastest gust recorded that day was 137 miles per hour. Most of the gusts had ranged between 110 and 135 miles per hour outside of the covered tree lines and trails. December 21 had been labeled the end of the world on the Mayan 2012 calendar, yet it brought pure beauty into my life and was labeled as an epic day on my Wildlife 2012 calendar, which I will remember for a lifetime.

Since we were all still alive and well here on Earth, Danielle and I spent the next night sitting beside a roaring wood stove that filled our living room with warmth and love as we enjoyed a bottle of red and a bottle of white wine while we listened to Hawaiian island music and wrapped Christmas gifts together.

The last gift that I wrapped up was going to be a twist for Danielle. After I finished winding a gold and red bow around the box like a madman and placed it under the tree, she asked me, "What is that mess of a wrapping job?" I said, "That, right there, is a surprise for you and me, my love. You can open that one up on New Year's Eve." She had a look of curiosity in her eye and then picked up the box and gave it a shake, asking, "What is it?" I said nothing and gave her a left eye wink.

The next morning was not your typical weather for the end of December in New England. There wasn't any snow on the ground, the sky was bright blue, and the birds were chirping. I bundled up Ava D. and Kiana and took them to the conservation trails down the road from our home to get some fresh air and exercise. I followed my two little angels all over this peaceful land, smiling and laughing as I witnessed Ava D. walk over a small wooden bridge that crossed over a babbling brook. Then I looked back to see Kiana standing at the end of the bridge, holding her hand out as she made a noise to get her big sister's attention. Ava D. walked back to help her as I stood silently in the backdrop, waiting to see what was going to happen next. Ava D. reached out with a helping hand and said, **"Come on, Kiana."** I watched two siblings in love walk side by side, holding on to one another as they crossed over the small wooden bridge in the woods. Talk about a proud moment watching your children!

Christmas Eve night had finally arrived, and Ricky Ricardo, the name of our Elf on the Shelf, appeared here and there in our home. That little red creep kept the children full of joy during the December holidays. Ava D. put out a glass of whole milk and some chocolate chip cookies for good old Saint Nick before we tucked in our big three-year-old toddler, who had the magical Christmas joy sparkling in her eyes.

Christmas morning started with quiet little footsteps walking slowly down the hallway. Then our bedroom door pushed open, and Ava D. looked at me smiling as she walked around the side of the bed and climbed up to snuggle beside her mommy. Shortly after, I rose with a morning stretch and walked down the hall to go wake up Kiana. Then the four of us went downstairs with Ava D. leading the way, still holding that sparkle of joy. I fired up the wood stove and embraced the meaning of living in the present moment as I watched the three most beautiful girls in my life on December 25.

Later that week, there was another storm moving in, and New Hampshire was going to get hit hard on Thursday and Friday. More snow meant more fun! So Friday morning Danielle and I woke up early and took the day to ourselves to enjoy the winter weather. We drove up to the state of Vermont to meet up with Marty Mar and a good dear friend of ours, who went by the name of Boo! She and Marty were like two peas in a pod, and Danielle and I were lucky to have them in our lives and couldn't wait to get up to their Vermont house and spend the day cruising around Killington Mountain Ski Resort on snowboards.

Spending the day in Vermont on a snowboard had cleared my mind of some unfinished business I had with "the Golden State." California had been a place that I felt was calling my name for quite some time now. That three-word question that ended up in a newspaper article way back in January 2012—"WILL HE SURVIVE?"—had not stopped lingering around in my thoughts and needed to be answered for me to continue with a clean slate.

When I told Danielle I had booked a flight to California for December 30, her eyes opened wide and said, "What do you mean? You're not going to spend New Year's Eve with me and the girls?" I started laughing and said, "Of course I am. I wouldn't miss the end of 2012 with you and the girls. I'll be back the morning of New Year's Eve. I fly out early on the thirtieth. I'm only spending four hours in California, and then I return home in the early a.m. on Sunday the thirty-first." Danielle asked, "What do you need to do in California with only four hours before you board another plane and fly six hours back to Boston?" I smiled and said, "I have to take care of something that is important to me."

Now, I had been throwing a lot at Danielle the last few months, but this time she was looking at me like I had lost my fucking mind. She asked me again, "Can you tell me what you're going out there for?" I was hoping she wouldn't ask me again, but she did. I told Danielle, and only her, what my plans were and asked her not to let anybody know that I was dipping out. After I finished telling her my plans, she looked me in the eye and actually said to me, **"You have completely lost your mind, David,** but I respect your reasoning." Then she shook her head with that smile I've seen a million times.

Once Danielle and I finished our conversation, we put the girls to bed, and her cell phone rang. It was her older brother, Eric. He asked if he could come over the following night to practice presenting a speech that he had been working on. They planned it so he could have dinner with me and Danielle and spend some time with his nieces, Ava D. and Kiana, before they went to bed. That meant he would be showing up to our home on the night of December 29. I told Danielle that sounded good since we hadn't seen him in a while, and the girls would love to see Uncle Eric.

The next morning I fired up both wood stoves in our home, Danielle made a big breakfast for our family of four, and then we all sat around a warm living room playing with some of the girls' new Christmas toys. I tossed on a wool jacket and slipped into some high-top rubber boots and went for a walk out back near the pond. It was a strange walk. It felt like I had climbed out of a rabbit hole or something once I passed the end of the barn and headed toward the pond. The weather of my backyard had felt exactly the same right before *Survivor*, the game, was put on hold and survivor, real life, had called my name. I remembered how I had made my first travel into the city to start a new life on March 5, and that's when I truly believe I may have fallen into a rabbit hole, and everything after that first chemo drip became one hell of a good trip.

Then, as I continued walking toward the pond, and with only sixty hours left until our grandfather clock struck midnight, I looked to my right and saw the wooden bench I had spent hours sitting on the past year and started thinking about how crazy it's going to be replaying all the footage to learn more about who I was and what the year had taught me about life. I walked right up to the edge of the pond and stood there, speechless, as I looked into the eyes of a wooden gnome that I had carved about a year ago and that Ava D. had named Willy the Wizard.

Nevertheless, I truly had never let go of the game; I created my own real-life show. It had become me versus the world, and like every *Survivor* game played, all you needed was strategy, skill, hard work, and a little bit of good old luck. Then it's up to the viewers—the audience that has been created over time. It's the fans that get to decide if you have shined brightly enough to earn victory. That would also be the determining factor for my own survivor project. I told myself I was going to give it my all. I had no idea who my audience would be or if they would even care, but I set my sights on the world as my target. My goal was to make a positive impact on my own mental health with a mission to help others along the way while pushing open a door for myself as a writer. I walked back up to my home with my head held high, focused on putting an end to the question "Will he survive?"

Danielle and I spent the rest of the afternoon playing with the girls as we waited for Uncle Eric to arrive. Danielle mentioned to me that her brother heard another really big snowstorm was moving in and was going to hit Massachusetts and New Hampshire in a few hours and then snow all through the night. I was a little concerned with the news about the forecast. I didn't have that much time to spare on my travels in the upcoming hours. But Mother Nature does what she wants, and time is the only way to tell what the outcome will be.

Eric arrived and said he had already hit some fresh snow on his way to our home. During supper the snow began to fly in our neck of the woods, and the forecast seemed to be right on point. The flakes were big, falling and accumulating quickly. Uncle Eric spent some time playing with Ava D. and Kiana before it was their bedtime. He then asked, "Do you mind if I spend the night since the weather is getting so bad so I don't have to make the hour commute back into Mass during the storm?"

My heart kind of dropped when he said he was spending the night because I had to leave the house at two thirty the next morning to catch my flight out of Boston Logan Airport. I didn't want anybody to know that I was dipping out for a quick trip to California. Danielle and I both said of course he could stay the night. After the girls went to bed, Danielle and I sat on the couch while Eric got set up in front of us to speak. Twenty-five minutes into Eric's speech, I felt like getting off the couch and running through a wall or something. I was so fired up inside with inspiration, but I stayed collected and seated during Eric's speech.

He had been taking courses through a company called Landmark, which offered personal development programs. The material that he was presenting in front of us was all about doing something that is important in life. I was having a hard time holding myself together because I was about to be airborne on a flight to create and accomplish exactly what he was touching on, in only a few short hours, and he had no clue what my intentions even were or where I was headed. The timing of his speech was epic for me, and that's what life is all about—pulling each other up—and Uncle Eric was giving me ten fingers to reach up and touch the top of the world. But at the same time, it was hard to sit there, restless, and listen to him preach about conquering a vision.

My adrenaline had become so intense that I didn't even know what Eric was saying anymore. I had drifted out of reality and onto a new road, and all the lights were green, and in every direction all signs read, "Dreams This Way." **I was in tunnel vision, and the light was shining bright!**

At the end of Eric's presentation, I took a couple of deep breaths, stayed calm and collected, and asked him if he could please leave his keys out or if he wouldn't mind moving his car before he crashed for the night. He looked at me strangely and said, "I'm going to be leaving early in the morning, David." I smiled and then looked at Danielle as a grin grew on her face, and then I looked back at Eric and said, "I'm getting up at two thirty—are you leaving before that?" He quickly said, "Where the hell are you going at that hour in a snowstorm?" I told him, "I have a flight to catch out of Boston."

Eric asked again, "Where you going?" So I answered, "I'm going to California for a few hours, but I'll be back before the New Year." Eric then asked, "What are you doing in California for only a few hours?" I smiled and said, "I can't talk about it right now because I have not done it yet, but I will tell you my reasoning when the time is right, OK?"

He looked at me in a way that he had never looked at me before and slowly answered, "OK." I never even laid my head down that night. I watched the snowfall out my bedroom window, lying in my bed beside Danielle, with my eyes wide open, listening to plow trucks scrape on by our home and feeling stoked as ever about my future. The only thing that was a concern for me was the heavy snow dumping from the sky. I did not have much time to spare and couldn't afford a big delay or cancelation of my flight due to the weather.

Ring-a-ding-ding-ding! The two-thirty alarm went off, and I jumped in the shower for a quick wake-up rinse. I gave Danielle, Ava D., and Kiana a kiss, and then grabbed my backpack and made my way into a driveway full of snow. I cleaned off my truck, stuck the key in the ignition, and headed to the freeway in the middle of a December blizzard!

There were state plow trucks across all lanes on the freeway, making for slow travel into the city, but I was still looking OK timewise so I cranked the radio and held on firm to a ten-and-two grip in the southbound lane. I finally pulled into the airport, parked my truck, tossed my backpack over my shoulders, went through the security process, and boarded the plane that was bringing me to my destination.

I tucked my pack into the overhead compartment and sank into my seat. I was back in relaxation mode. Then an announcement carried throughout the aircraft. There was too much snow and ice on the wings and engines of the plane to take off. I took a deep breath and then conked out in my seat. I was woken up by another announcement, and I looked at my watch to see I had fallen asleep for one hour. The aircraft was still in the parked position. This second announcement over the intercom let all passengers know that we were good for takeoff.

As soon as I touched down in San Diego, I flagged a cab ride to Pacific Beach. The cab driver started with small talk and asked me where I was from. I told him north of Boston, and then he asked me how long I was staying in California. I laughed and said four hours. Once I got out of the cab, I got a quick bite to eat near the boardwalk and then headed straight for the salt and sand. I found a quiet spot to sit and relax while looking out at the Pacific Ocean as I began thinking about what I had actually even come to this Golden State to accomplish. There were a few people at the end of a jetty to my left, looking out at a view that seemed to go on forever.

The tide was coming in, and the sun was slowly starting to set as the sky began filling up with bright, vibrant colors. The people at the end of the jetty had turned around and started making their way back to the sandy shore. I stood up, brushed the sand off my pants, and began stepping my way closer toward the jetty as foamy, salty ocean water continuously flowed up near my feet as I walked past scattered seaweed. I was on my way to a spot that I believed was going to help me complete my survivorship in both the game and real life. I was about to live the quote "Kill two birds with one stone."

As I made my way, stepping and leaping from rock to rock, moving closer to a view that seemed endless, I began exploding inside with feelings of joy, peace, love, hope, humility, kindness, empathy, and most of all TRUTH in who I was as a human being as well as a son, husband, father, and friend to everybody that I loved and respected in my life.

At the end of the jetty I took a moment to lose myself in the California sunset and then pulled out the card with the stone in it that my godparents had given me after a night filled with fireworks celebrating the Fourth of July. A few weeks after I received the card, my uncle Mark had finally explained to me why the stone was part of the gift, and more so why it was inspiring to him. He told me he had picked up a black stone while walking alone on the beaches of California, back when his son, my first cousin, Captain Christopher Mark George, was in active duty in Afghanistan as a mine sweeper. My uncle told me he would carry the stone around with him, and every time he would think about Christopher, he would take the stone out and rub it in his hands for his own inspiration.

My uncle Mark and auntie Mary were back in California, walking the beaches once again in early spring, when I started going through chemotherapy. He explained to me that he had picked up another stone and held onto it when I was going through one of the largest battles in my own life. My uncle said he was trying to decide when it would be the best time to pass the stone off to me, which ended up being the Fourth of July. The card that I was holding in my hand, at the end of the jetty on December 30, explained in writing that he wanted me to hold on to this stone for my own inspiration, and I was to return it back to the beach when I felt the time was right.

More than they will ever know, my godparents had filled me with hope and faith after they had passed that card into my hands. The black stone did more than become superstitious to my well-being. It inspired me to stay focused and gave me clarity on one thing and one thing only.

My big dream!

I began rubbing the black stone in between my thumb and index finger as my eyes looked deep into the Golden State's sunset. I closed my eyes tightly and made the same wish that I had been making since I was a young boy bumping down the road in that big old green dump truck, past Robert Frost's farm. I also thought about the magic show I'd seen, performed by a walking legend, David Copperfield, in Boston, and the impact it had on me, especially during his last magic trick of the night. He told a story about how if you wanted something bad enough in life, all you had to do was never stop dreaming or wishing for that one great thing, and one day it would come true.

Since that moment on, for the past nineteen years, every birthday candle I have blown out, wishbone broken, clock read at 11:11, eyelash blown away, or coin tossed into a fountain—I focused on my dream. Anytime at all that I had the opportunity to drift off into a dreamworld or make a wish, it was the same strong vision over and over again, and I have yet to tell a soul my lifelong dream. I've always been a strong believer in magic, and with belief, we all have the ability to trick ourselves about what we are able to become in a world filled with freedom and possibilities.

Once I opened my eyes, I threw that smooth black stone of inspiration into a sky that was limitless. I became blinded by the golden sunset; I never even saw the stone hit the ocean water, and maybe it never did. Gravity doesn't usually fail but neither does MAGIC nor yourself, if you believe.

Both birds were knocked down with one stone, and that three-word question from the newspaper article was finally put to rest with a resounding YES! The only thing I had left to do was make it back home safely to Danielle and my girls so I could complete my goal of documenting my life right up until the end of the year and feel 100 percent fulfilled on everything that I have worked toward during this epic life-changing year.

Shortly after I returned the stone to the beach, the sky became covered in thick, dark gray clouds with heavy winds. The colorful sunset disappeared completely within minutes. **I had the wildest vibe throughout my body** as I stood patiently waiting to see what was going to happen next. A few minutes of strong gusts continuously blew over the ocean as the sky darkened, and then it stopped instantly, and piercing golden-orange rays of light shined onto the splashing waves below.

I headed back up to the boardwalk to flag down a cab ride back to the airport. I stopped before my last step off the Pacific Beach and placed my GoPro in the sand, facing what was once again a California golden sunset. I ended up slowly walking back down to the water's edge for one more good look at where I believed my big dream came true!

Once my feet were back on top of pavement, in my search for a cab, I noticed the sky quickly fill up with thick, gray overcast conditions and let out some fast-flying rain. I let my hands turn over with my palms facing up as I closed my eyes and then lifted my chin high to the sky. All I could do at this point was once again feel. We've been told that raindrops are good luck and that's all I felt, standing in a state of "Eureka!"

I flagged down a cab, made it to the San Diego Airport, and traveled back to Boston. After a safe landing it was back on the freeway, heading northbound back to the homestead.

That night I cooked up a nice meal for my family, and then Danielle and I played with our two little girls until they couldn't even hold their eyes open anymore. We tucked them both in, wished them a "Happy New Year," and said, "We love you," and then closed their bedroom door quietly and headed downstairs to spend time with each other. It was finally time for Danielle to open up that last Christmas gift I had wrapped up for New Year's Eve. It was the game Twister.

Danielle put on some reggae music, and I popped our first bottle of champagne as Danielle placed her right hand on red in a game of strip Twister as the clock ticked away closer to the end of the final chapter. With only seconds left counting down until the big hand struck twelve, Danielle and I put a hold on our game as I got ready to pop another bottle, and then while looking into the love of my life's eyes, our granddaddy clock let out BONG! Then I popped the cork, followed by another BONG! BONG! BONG! As my lips pressed hard into Danielle's, there was another BONG! BONG! We held on tightly to one another as the clock rang out six more loud melodies throughout our home, putting an end to 2012 as Danielle and I stayed tightly together as I drifted into a moment of thankfulness.

The year 2012 was amazing, astonishing, awesome, breathtaking, sensational, remarkable, spectacular, and straight up simply marvelous! Not the year that ended the world, but definitely the end of my book.

My lifelong dream was to write a book
While making art out of my life.
And like any artist in the world,
You are nothing until you are REAL!

The reason why I was able to turn my reality into a dream come true was because I never gave up. I stayed true to building a lifestyle off those four phrases that had been ingrained into my brain by the four men in my life that I respected and loved with all my heart. Mark, Peter, Paul, and good old Ricky Roy.

First, work will mess up your entire life! So I chose to slowly put aside what I did to make a living during 2012. Second, you're only successful if you do what you enjoy in life! With work put aside, I was able to focus on only what I truly enjoyed. Third, do everything you say you're going to do in life! I told myself that I was going to film myself day in and day out until the end of the year while staying disciplined to my word. Fourth, **sky's the limit!** After hearing that phrase over and over again as a youth, I chose to think positively and follow my heart no matter what kind of challenges I encountered during the year of 2012.

The one person that has inspired me most, about dreaming more than others think is practical and expecting more than others think is possible, will always be the love of my life, my wife, Danielle R. George. Since 2004, I have been telling her that I was going to write a book, never mentioning what kind, but anytime those words came out of my mouth, she would say, "David, you can't write a book if you don't read books. You hate to read. So how do you plan on writing a book?" My response was always, "You don't have to read books to write books; all you need to do is know how to live."

My first book is dedicated to Danielle.

I would also like to take the time to thank anybody that chose to follow through with investing in my life story. Whether you read, watched, or listened to *The Year It All Made Sense.*

If you say you're going to do something, then do it. There is no other reason why we fail in life other than the individual choosing to give up. Whether it's in how we conduct ourselves in pleasure or business, we own who we are and what we choose to leave behind for others.

So make it a win-win and keep on dreaming!

God bless

&

Peace out to the world!

Acknowledgments

First and foremost I want to thank my wife, Danielle, and our two beautiful daughters, Ava D. & Kiana.

Weasel.

My grandparents, G & G Siopes, Papa Bill, Pepe Roy, and in loving memory of Dorothy George, Donald George, and Memere.

My mother, Diane Marie. My father, Paul William. My sister Jennifer Marie. My sister Amanda Lee.

My godparents, Mark & Mary George.

Pete & Phillis George, Richard & Phillis Roy, Linda Simpson, Tina George, Brian & Debbie Dumais, and Auntie Mabel.

My cousins Melissa, Kara, Desiree, Christopher, Keri, Nicholas, Ashley, Christina, Jared, Chelsea, Dillon, Caron, Adam, and Elizabeth.

My niece, Aliya Grace, and nephews, Tyler Michael and Mason Paul.

My in-laws, Henry & Demetra Roberge.

My brothers-in-law, Shane Wakeen and Eric Roberge.

David & Diane Sollars.

Jeffrey McGurren, Derek Wakeen.

CP, Uncle Buck, Black Bird, Rocco, Sandy Kattar (for my four wooden prayer bracelets), *Kylee Kattar*, Calvin Kattar, Jose Madera, Kaddie & Brian, Lindsay Santoro, Jenny, Virginia, Holly, Ethan Conley, Markus Sebastiano, Dawn Kingston, John & Maureen Saba, Kim Whalen, Auntie Allison & Alex, Jen Samiotes, Dr. Richard Lee, Tai, all my nurses and doctors, MGH, Danna Farber, and Brigham & Women's Hospital.

To good neighbors: Julie, Jen, Julie & Jimmy Knox, the Ashfords, and Roderick & Pam and the boys.

Stacey D. Atkinson, Kevin Callahan, Patricia MacDonald, Kevin Attar, George "the Governor" Blaisdell, Barry Greenwood, Coach Rob, Jay Atkinson, the NH Boxing and Wrestling Commission, Rockingham Park, Ed Callahan, Lynne Snierson, New England MMA, Chris Konalas, Kevin Pricci, Ed Carr, John Fain, Steve Rita, Kevin "the Ref" MacDonald, Matt Peterson, Jeff Thompson & Thompson Auto Group, Matt Linquist & Cleary Creative, Kathy Chadwick & Wharf Industries, Tom Obrey, Chris Martin, Slim Jimmy, Rockey L., Atlantic Crane, All Pro, Mark Shook, Jason Cyr, Danny Lagori, John H., Dan Wells, S&H Tree Service, Windham Tree Service, Rich Wells, Joe Turner, Livingston Family Tree, and in loving memory of Joshua W. Dumont.

Patrick Mackallagat, Lori DelliColli & Chris Harrington.

Caitlin Moore with the game show *Survivor*!

An enormous thank you to all who sent me a card during my time at MGH.

Thank you to everyone who supported the Kickstarter campaign.